MATILDA LIAR!

MATILDA LIAR!

by Debbie Isitt

WARNER CHAPPELL PLAYS

LONDON

A Time Warner Company

MATILDA LIAR!
First published in 1994
by Warner Chappell Plays Ltd
129 Park Street, London W1Y 3FA

ISBN 0 85676 214 8

For my sisters, Jacqueline and Sally

MATILDA LIAR! was first produced by the Snarling Beasties Theatre Company as a co-production with Warwick Arts Centre, and first performed at the Arts Centre in October, 1994. In November 1994 the production transferred to the Tricycle Theatre, London. The cast was as follows:

MATILDA	Rebecca Jackson
FATHER	Peter Hamilton
MOTHER	Sue White
MICHAEL	Morgan Edwards
FIONA	Lucy Richardson

Directed by Debbie Isitt
Designed by Gary Tanner
Stage Managed by Nigel Mousley
Original Music by Barb Jungr

FOREWORD

As a child I read with fear and excitement Belloc's *Matilda, Who Told Such Dreadful Lies*. Perhaps, like many children, I identified with the little horror who wanted more excitement in her life.

I recall telling all kinds of lies to squirm my way out of trouble, to liven up mundane events, and to fantasise myself as a hero in incredible tales of good fortune gained with honour.

Pretending in life is something we all do, and those of us who particularly enjoy it often opt for a life in the theatre. As soon as I arrived at acting school I discovered that pretending was out and truth was in. It was not enough to fake — one had to feel it for real in the moment. The lie had to be true. It is dificult to attempt a play about lies and truth without understanding this.

Matilda Liar! is a funny and dark cautionary tale. It demands energy, commitment and a level of realism that stops it escalating into pantomime. This is a play about how we function inside the family and although it is often cruel, one must never lose sight of the love in the play. Their love for each other is obscured by anxieties and the protection racket they are caught up in, but it is there in their rantings and ravings and ultimately in their grief and their loss. A comedy and a tragedy — just like life.

Debbie Isitt
1994

DESIGN NOTES

MATILDA'S room is encased in a spiral tower of steps. It is bare with a wooden floor. Behind her, and attached to the structure of the staircase hangs a huge gilt mirror towering above her. The mirror is fairy-tale in style and reflects her actions.

The spiral staircase has steps leading to her room and continuing off it towards the heavens. The whole structure is distressed with purple, blue and lilac paint subtly shaded to create a gothic feel. The staircase provides shelving. In the upper part of the spiral MATILDA'S books sit in the shelves. They are all dressed in metallic paper in blue and purple and pink. They twinkle when the lights hit them. The lower part of the spiral the shelves house a fish tank belonging to MICHAEL and magazines belonging to FATHER. Encased in the lower part of the staircase sits FIONA on her swivel chair, hidden for much of the action inside the structure itself. She is revealed only when she swings out for her scenes. A painted aluminium fire ladder is attached to the front of the structure and is extended to its full height during the "burning" scene. There lies near it a metal bath full of water, catching a drip from the upper part of the structure. The bath is on wheels.

Downstage there is a dining table and chairs and a sitting area which can be represented by a couple of the dining chairs. Buried into the back of the staircase structure and hidden by a blue velvet curtain sit the props. These consist of party hats that look like crowns, paper plates and cups, brightly coloured balloons, chocolate cakes, brightly packaged Pandora's box for pass the parcel, etc.

The style of the piece is a mixture of the gothic cautionary tale and the glittering fairy-tale. The characters dress in the gothic cautionary tale style, although they must have a contemporary feel.

MATILDA wears a childlike purple velvet party dress above the knees but over it a scruffy cardigan in scarlet red. Her coat is also above her knees and in scarlet, images of Little Red Riding Hood and other dark tales should be evoked. A wedding dress hangs alone in MATILDA'S room, a constant image of her waiting for her prince.

PROLOGUE

Distant thunder rumbles. The space is in blackness. The whispering of MATILDA'S *name fills the space. She opens a large book with a bulb shining from its pages and out of the blackness her face lights up eerily. She is in her room at the top of a spiral staircase. She reads aloud from the book.*

MATILDA   Dear Marjorie,

When emotions rule my head and people rule my life, when I'm feeling nearly dead because I've lost my lust for life, when I can't sleep 'cause I'm worried and I'm worried so I can't sleep, so my energy is sapped from all the secrets that I keep. And I wish that I could be myself there's so much I could do, but instead of being happy I just feel all shit and crappy, and there's no one else to talk to, so that's why I write to you. I'm frightened of so many things, I have so many doubts, I'm so worried about Matilda and the fire that burned her house and I know it's just a silly kiddie's rhyme but I feel as though I'm running out of time, I have to get away from Mum and Dad, so I just wondered Marjorie, am I going mad?

Matilda.

(She closes the book and lies down in darkness. The family appear in shadow. Their voice-over is heavily amplified. Sound effects and lighting give nightmarish quality as the poem fills her dreams.)

FAMILY   Matilda told such dreadful lies
It made one gasp and stretch one's eyes
Her aunt who from her earliest youth
Had kept a strict regard for truth
Attempted to believe Matilda
The effort very nearly killed her

For once towards the close of day
Matilda growing tired of play
And finding she was left alone
Went tip-toe to the telephone
And summoned immediate aid
Of London's noble fire brigade

Within an hour the gallant band
Were pouring on every hand
They galloped roaring through the town
"Matilda's house is burning down"

Until Matilda's aunt succeeded
In showing them they were not needed
It happened that a few weeks later
Her aunt was off to the theatre

That night a fire did break out
You should have heard Matilda shout
You should have heard her scream and bawl
And throw the window up and call

For every time she shouted "Fire!"
They only answered "Little Liar!"
And therefore when her aunt returned
Matilda and the house were burned
Matilda and the house were burned
Matilda and the house were . . .

(MATILDA *sits bolt up in a sweat as all sounds cut.
She has woken from her dream to hear voices
coming from downstairs. The light shifts to reveal*
MOTHER, FATHER *and* MICHAEL *sitting around the
table. The tension builds.*)

ACT ONE

MOTHER   It's not as if I haven't warned her
              It's not as if I haven't tried

FATHER   It's that gang she hangs around with Mother
              She couldn't help it if she lied
              They influence her moral judgement

They lead her on, they make her bad
It isn't our fault it isn't hers

MICHAEL   Don't make excuses for her Dad
She's always been a lying cow

FATHER   Now don't let's have another row

MICHAEL   You just won't see it will you though
You just won't get it through your head
She's horrible, Matilda is
I've had enough I'm back to bed

MOTHER   Stay where you are Michael!
Please Frank, you've got to see
She's turned into a little beast

FATHER   Well what do you want me to do?

MOTHER   Take her to a Catholic Priest

MICHAEL   They'd exorcize the little demon
If they'd let her in the church

FATHER   Don't blaspheme about your sister

MICHAEL   Go into her room and search!
You're bound to find some drugs in there
She should be taken into care

FATHER   Maybe if she joined the choir?

MOTHER   They wouldn't take Matilda Liar
In St Martha's angel choir
You're her father, its up to you
Give her a bloody good talking to!

(FATHER *gives in and moves cautiously towards*
MATILDA'S *bedroom . The rest of the family*
shadow him up the spiral staircase.)

FATHER   Matilda . . .

(*No answer.*)

Matilda . . .

(*No answer.*)

MOTHER   MATILDA!

MATILDA   What?

FATHER   I'd like a word with you.

MATILDA   What?

FATHER   Your mother's got something to say.

MOTHER   I have not! Your father wants a little chat.

MATILDA   What about?

MOTHER   About you.

MATILDA   What about me?

MOTHER   About you and your behaviour.

MATILDA   What about me and my behaviour?

MOTHER   Oh for God's sake Frank, talk to her!

FATHER   I've got nothing to say.

MATILDA   Well can I go back to bed then?

MOTHER }   Yes.
FATHER   No.

MATILDA   But I don't feel well.

FATHER   What's wrong?

MATILDA   I've got an ear-ache.

FATHER   Well I can't talk to her if she's got an ear-ache, can I? She won't be able to hear me. You go to bed, Tillie.

(*The family descend the staircase, defeated.*)

MOTHER   An ear-ache is it, in which ear?

FATHER   An ear-ache means she cannot hear.

MICHAEL   A headache is what she's given me.

FATHER   Let's leave it then 'til we've had our tea.

(MATILDA *is left alone and feeling irritable. She speaks aloud to her imaginary mirror.*)

MATILDA   Dear Marjorie,

Thank you for your last letter, I was very interested to hear about new Oxy Zit, that spot on my chin has almost completely disappeared now, except for a yellow head which should burst any day. I don't suppose there is anything as powerful for removing excess facial hair as I read an advertisement in a teenage magazine about unwanted feminine hair cream. It didn't make it clear whether you can use it on your face and I am getting worried about growth above my top lip as the way things stand on the boyfriend scene a moustache could prove disastrous. I have also acquired a recent spare tyre bringing the total up to three. I've asked my mother to stop feeding me but she says I need my strength, although she won't specify what I need it for. Please Marjorie, if there is anything you could send me that might help attract the man I want to marry I would be eternally grateful. Please don't write back and tell me that beauty is in the eye of the beholder and don't send me any more literature on anorexia, please just send me something that will make me thin and beautiful.

Yours, Matilda.

(MOTHER *is approaching the top of the stairs so* MATILDA *turns away.*)

MOTHER   Matilda, can I come in?

MATILDA   No, go away.

MOTHER   I want to talk to you.

MATILDA   Just leave me alone can't you?

MOTHER   Come on Matilda, please?

MATILDA   Go away!

(MOTHER, *hurt and angry, joins* FATHER *in the sitting room, where he is leafing through cruise ship holiday magazines.* MICHAEL *sits at the table building up the inners of an elaborate fish tank.* MATILDA *listens to her parents.*)

MOTHER   She wouldn't let me in.

FATHER   She'll come out in her own time.

MOTHER   She's probably reading those stupid books.

FATHER   So what if she is, what harm can it do?

MOTHER   She should be applying for jobs.

FATHER   Don't rush her, let her do it in her own time.

MOTHER   She doesn't know anything Frank, she's got no common sense, no skills.

FATHER   She's alright, what does she need common sense for?

MOTHER   Because I know what will happen!

FATHER   What do you know? You're always looking on the black side, she's got her whole life ahead of her, you know nothing.

MOTHER   I got another letter from Fiona.

FATHER   Did you? Did she mention the kids?

MOTHER   She says they're both fine.

FATHER   I bet they're right little tearaways just like their grandad.

MOTHER   I wouldn't know.

FATHER   (*changing subject*) Why don't you have a flick through some of these brochures I brought home, choose where you want to go on your second honeymoon.

MOTHER   I haven't had my first one yet!

FATHER   Well choose two places then, I'll take you on both!

MOTHER   I don't want to look at them Frank, I don't want to see places I can't go to.

FATHER   Well that's what they're there for, so you can choose somewhere!

MOTHER   I've chosen a million times and I'm still here.

FATHER   Well you have just got to be patient my dear.

     (*Music.* MATILDA *purposefully makes her way downstairs to join her family.* MOTHER *and* FATHER *look up as she enters.*)

MOTHER   What job?

MATILDA   I told you I went for that interview last week — the manager's position at the bank.

FATHER   Fantastic!

MATILDA   £20,000 a year, I start on Monday.

FATHER   Fantastic!

MOTHER   How can a school-leaver get a manager's position?

FATHER   She's bright Matilda is, she could get any job.

MOTHER   Where's the letter then?

MATILDA   What letter?

MOTHER   The letter offering you the manager's position.

MATILDA   They're going to put it in writing next week.

MOTHER   But you start on Monday.

FATHER   Start on Monday. Fantastic!

MOTHER   Shut up Frank.

MATILDA   If you don't believe me ring them up.

MOTHER   Alright I will.

FATHER   There's no need for that.

MOTHER   There is a need Frank, she's got to learn.

MATILDA   Learn what?

MOTHER   Pass me the phone.

MATILDA   No.

MOTHER   Oh, why not?

MATILDA   Because I turned it down, I don't want to work
            for the bank.

FATHER   Of course she doesn't want to work for the bank.

MOTHER   What does she want to do then, Frank? Fly to the
            moon on a space shuttle or run the country —
            would that suit her better — you could do it
            together on a job share!

MATILDA   I'm not going to do anything.

MOTHER   Oh well, good luck to you then, you'll need it.

MATILDA   I mean I'm getting married.

FATHER   Of course she is.

MOTHER   And who to this time?

MATILDA   A man.

MOTHER   Well that's something I suppose.

FATHER   Matilda will surprise us all, won't you pet?

MATILDA   I'm pregnant.

MOTHER   Don't be ridiculous.

MATILDA   The father and I are getting married.

FATHER   Fantastic!

MOTHER   And who is the father?

MATILDA   You don't know him.

MOTHER   No and neither do you because he doesn't exist!

FATHER   There's a film on in a minute, shall we watch it?

MATILDA   I haven't decided if I'm keeping it.

MOTHER   Well I'm sure the infant will miraculously disappear just like all the others have, I'm surprised you've any insides left the amount of short term pregnancies you've had. I don't suppose the phantom father will be popping round to meet us, I expect he'll miraculously disappear as well!

MATILDA   He can hardly just pop round from the other side of the world can he? Just to meet you.

MOTHER   Oh very convenient, another continent! So we can't question him like we could your doctor and your teacher and the poor old man at the post office. At least you've spared us all the humiliation of that.

FATHER   Look, the film's starting!

MATILDA   I'm going to book myself into the clinic. You don't deserve a grandchild.

MOTHER   I wish I'd booked myself into the clinic 'cause I certainly don't deserve you!

(MATILDA *has stormed off.*)

FATHER   Do you have to upset her like that?

MOTHER   She upsets me Frank, what about that?

(MICHAEL *looks up from his fish tank.*)

MICHAEL   You should have strangled her at birth.

(MATILDA *in her room, stands before her mirror
in a rage. She acts out the story with much
emotion as music builds (Richard Strauss 'Great
Longing'), and the story is clearly connected to
*MATILDA's *feelings about her mother and father.*)

MATILDA   And on the top of the cliff stood a mighty castle
with huge turrets and high windows, the waves
beneath it crashed onto its sides and in it lived a
vain and wicked queen obsessed with her own
beauty. "Mirror, mirror, on the wall, who is the
fairest of them all"? The mirror always answered
"You are majesty, you are the fairest in the land",
but one day the mirror did not answer so.
"Somewhere in a far-off wood a young girl lives,
much fairer than you, her skin is white as snow,
her eyes as blue as sapphires, her hair as black as
ebony, her lips as red as the ripest cherry, her
delicate hands are soft as silk and she is beautiful
beyond compare, so beautiful, men weep to look
upon her, they long to touch her satin cheeks
with bones so finely chiselled, they long to caress
her soft and slender neck and nuzzle their faces
into her warm flesh, she is fresh and innocent
and pure as the purest dove. Her spirit flies and
everything she touches comes alive, for she is
beauty rare." "What is her name?" the queen
commanded. "Name the girl — she who you say
is fairer than me. Speak. Speak her name! Her
name I tell you!" "Matilda!" answered the mirror.
"Matilda is her name". "MATILDA!" screamed
the wicked queen, turning green with envy. And
she ordered a huntsman to her court. "I want you
to go far into the forest, there you will find a girl

with skin like snow, eyes like sapphires, hair like ebony and lips like cherry — her name is — Matilda. Kill her and bring me her heart! Now go!" The huntsman took his sword into his hand and fought his way into the forest. On finding Matilda he was so enamoured of her beauty that he could not find it in his heart to kill her, but fearing the queen's mighty wrath found a stag and ripped out its heart. Balancing the heart carefully on the edge of his sword he hurried back through the forest and delivered it to the queen. "Is this is the heart of Matilda?" "Yes", lied the huntsman. "Ha! Ha! Ha! Ha! Ha! Ha! Ha!" laughed the wicked queen "Now I am once again the fairest in this land!" Meanwhile in the forest a handsome prince on horseback saw Matilda playing. On sight he almost fainted for he had ne'er seen such a beauty. They looked into each other's eyes and danced and kissed and laughed and when he tasted her cherry lips he knew he was in love. He asked her name and left her, vowing to return and claim her as his princess. Matilda waited in the forest for her lover to return and she longed for him, how she longed for him, how she would embrace him, wrap her legs around him, ride him side-saddle, legs a straddle, ravage him and savage him, oh he'll be coming soon, he'll be coming soon, coming soon, coming, coming, coming . . .

(FATHER *interrupts her, entering her room.*)

FATHER   What are you doing?

MATILDA   Reading — so get out!

FATHER   Your mother doesn't like you reading those books.

MATILDA   Well if she stayed out of my room she wouldn't know what I was reading and then she wouldn't have to worry about it!

FATHER   You know what she's like, she's got no imagination.

MATILDA   What do you want?

FATHER   I just thought . . . oh, look at this, I love this one.
            Sleeping Beauty. It's my favourite. My mother
            used to read it to us when we were little. Which
            one's your favourite?

MATILDA   Snow White.

FATHER   And me, Snow White.

MATILDA   You just said it was that one.

FATHER   And Snow White. Great minds think alike, eh?
            Great minds think alike . . . ?

            (*She does not respond.*)

            I'm so excited about the wedding.

MATILDA   What wedding?

FATHER   What wedding! Your wedding. I won't let you
            down, you'll have any dress you ask for —
            original, magical, white as snow.

MATILDA   Thanks Dad, but I don't want white, I want pearl.

FATHER   Pearl? Ok pearl, if that's what you want. In
            purest silk.

MATILDA   I want satin, not silk!

FATHER   But it creases!

MATILDA   I can hire someone to hold it straight.

FATHER   The car must be a —

MATILDA   A Ferrari.

FATHER   A white Ferrari.

MATILDA   No! A red one.

FATHER   A red Ferrari for a wedding car? . . . And the
            bridesmaids will be in pale pink and all the gents
            in top hats. I want everyone there to see you walk
            down that aisle.

MATILDA   Not too many people.

FATHER   The world and his friends — in the cathedral, not
            the church and a five-star hotel with a five course
            menu and a horse and carriage to take you there.

MATILDA   I'll be driving the Ferrari.

FATHER   You'll be sitting in the carriage and the confetti
            will be flowing and I'll arrange the honeymoon.

MATILDA   But honeymoons are meant to be secret.

FATHER   Well I'm not going to tell anyone, it'll be our
            secret.

MATILDA   I don't want it to be our secret, it's got nothing to
            do with you!

FATHER   It's got everything to do with me, I'll be paying
            for it!

MATILDA   Well how will you afford it?

FATHER   You sound just like your mother, never mind the
            cost, you just concentrate on looking lovely. You
            want your old dad to be proud of you don't you?

MATILDA   Yes, its just . . .

FATHER   Well then, that's settled, a special wedding for a
            special princess.

            (*He gets up and walks over to* MATILDA'S
            imaginary mirror.)

            Oh yes, you're a good looking bugger, Frank
            Keen.

(Lights shift to the dining area where MICHAEL *is still fiddling with the fish tank.* MOTHER *enters.)*

MOTHER   Are you alright Michael?

MICHAEL   Yes fine, thank you.

MOTHER   Do you have to keep fiddling with that fish tank — can't you go upstairs and talk to your sister!

MICHAEL   I'm not talking to a liar.

MOTHER   You could be getting on with your life by now, not still at home at your age. What must people think?

MICHAEL   Who cares what people think? I've told you Mother, I've got a life, here with you and Dad. That's the only life I want.

MOTHER   Couldn't you just try again, let me phone her, invite her to tea, I'm sure, if we explained to her about Matilda Elaine would come round, she's a sensible girl . . .

MICHAEL   Shut up Mother! Shut it!

MOTHER   I'm sorry Michael.

MICHAEL   What's he doing up there anyway?

MOTHER   I sent him up to talk to her.

MICHAEL   Well he wants to be careful, these days fathers who visit their daughter's bedrooms usually get a visit from Social Services shortly afterwards.

MOTHER   Don't say things like that Michael! She's got to be spoken to, she won't listen to me.

MICHAEL   Well what do you think he's going to say to her? He'll just pat her on the head like he always does, she'll never change. Never!

MOTHER   Well she's going to have to. Because I'm not living with her behaviour any more and she's not leaving this house until she learns how to behave.

(MOTHER *has left the room and is approaching the bottom of the staircase when* FATHER *bursts out of* MATILDA'S *room singing the wedding march.* MATILDA *hovers reluctantly behind him, wearing a wedding dress.* MOTHER *is horrified.*)

MOTHER   FOR GOD'S SAKE FRANK WHAT ARE YOU DOING?

FATHER   I'm rehearsing her for her big day, she looks lovely doesn't she? Aghhh! I can't stand it, I can't stand it, it's all doom and gloom and blackness. You bring me down with all your worry, I'm catching it I've got to hurry, Michael you will talk to Matilda, you've got to forgive and forget, Mother you'll leave her be and everyone WILL be happy, I'm not having this tension in the air, this misery that's everywhere, we'll forget about the sorrow caused a year ago tomorrow and we'll celebrate instead, we'll have a party, yes a PARTY and you'll all ENJOY yourselves and that's FINAL do you HEAR ME!?!!

(FATHER *in a rage storms off after* MOTHER. MATILDA *rips off her wedding dress, puts on her coat and runs downstairs to* MICHAEL.)

MATILDA   Michael why don't we get out now, before this stupid party? Pack your things we can be somewhere else by morning . . . Michael . . . Michael, come with me!

MOTHER   (*appearing suddenly*) Go with you where Matilda?

MATILDA   (*lying*) To the post office — I need some stamps.

MOTHER   I have some stamps you can have.

MATILDA   I need airmail.

MOTHER   What do you need airmail for?

MATILDA   You know very well.

MOTHER   Just stop this game Matilda and don't you dare leave this house!

(She has slammed out of the front door. MOTHER *puts her coat on as if to rush after her when* FATHER *appears.)*

FATHER   Was that Matilda going out?

MOTHER   Yes, and I'm going to get her back.

FATHER   Where's she gone?

MOTHER   To the post office.

FATHER   Oh, she could have got some brown paper for the Pass the Parcel.

MOTHER   Frank, the party is not the point. I don't want her going out.

FATHER   Oh take your coat off — take it off — you've got to let her have a bit of freedom.

*(*FATHER *rips* MOTHER'S *coat off her.)*

No more droopy mouths — smile, smile, smile! Come along now Michael, you too! I want you to smile, Son! Ok? SMILE! You know — SMILE! Come on lad, you can do it if you try, just SMILE! SMILE! SMILE!

*(*MICHAEL *attempts a smile.)*

THAT'S IT! TERRIFIC! You see, you can do it if you try.

MOTHER   Give me my coat back, Frank!

FATHER   Now you Mother — you smile.

MOTHER   GIVE ME MY COAT!

FATHER   You can have your coat back when you've smiled!

(MOTHER *grins hysterically and* FATHER *returns her coat.*)

There you are you see, you can both do it! Now then Michael you come and help me with the trimmings whilst your Mum makes us a nice cup of tea!

(FATHER *and* MICHAEL *exit as* MOTHER *puts her coat back on and sneaks out the door after* MATILDA. *Music. Blackout. Lights rise on* FIONA *who has glided into the frame on her swivel chair. She is lit with a special light that boxes her in. Soft music plays. She is on her mobile telephone, smoking.*)

FIONA   Yes, that's fine if you can make it but I've another meeting at twelve so it'll have to be a quickie I'm afraid. Ok Allie, see you then.

(*She hangs up and notices the audience.*)

Oh hello, you'll have to forgive me, it's just been one of those days today.

(*Phone rings.*)

Excuse me.

(*She picks it up.*)

Silver Screen, Fiona Keen speaking — Harry Hi, no, nope I can't do it Harry, you'll have to get Janet on the case, ok? Chow for now.

(*She hangs up.*)

Hot in here isn't it? And I forgot my body spray.

(*She sniffs her arm pits and grins.*)

Very unpleasant. It's good to be busy though, I can't stand being bored and my mother always said, "only the boring get bored" so I've been trying to be interesting ever since. Mothers are funny fish though — I'm 31 years old and I still can't smoke in front of mine. I'm terrified of going home now in case I forget and light up or shout obscenities over the dinner table, or just be myself really. Luckily, within half an hour of going home I've forgotten who I am anyway, having been reduced to a thirteen year old by both my parents who force me to eat my greens and wash my hands after going to the toilet. I mean I do wash my hands after going to the toilet — but not after a wee — just after a — never mind. Anyway, I've decided next time I'm going to take a piece of paper with me with my name written on it so I can remind myself of who I am, whenever they're not looking — FIONA KEEN: GROWN WOMAN. It was like escaping from Colditz leaving home. I had several unsuccessful attempts before I finally tunneled my way out through next door's garden . . . no, it was Richard who got me out — Richard rescued me — good old Dick . . .

(*Phone rings again.*)

Yes! Oh Dad! Hello . . . can you hold . . . on a sec, there's something on the stove. (*She stubbs out cigarette.*) Sorry Dad, its Richard's tea, yes I'm fine thanks, how are you . . . a year ago already? Oh hang on, the baby's crying.

(*She holds the phone away again and makes baby crying noises.*)

He just wanted his dum dums, of course I'm coping, I'm loving it . . . look Dad I can't talk for long, Richard will be home soon and you know how tired he gets. A party for who? . . . yes I would love to, of course I would! . . . I'm really really looking forward to it — I'll see you there then, brilliant, bye.

(*She slams phone down.*)

Shit. Shit. Shit. Shit. Shit.

(*Blackout. Lights rise on sitting room.* MOTHER *chases* MATILDA *into the house carrying a large wreath,* FATHER *chases after them trying to protect* MATILDA .)

MOTHER   (*dangerously waving wreath*) You go and tell her I'm alive!! I'm warning you Matilda, go and tell her NOW!

MATILDA   No.

MOTHER   DO AS YOU ARE TOLD!

FATHER   Please Matilda just go and say you made a little mistake, you got confused.

MATILDA   No.

MOTHER   I'm going to kill her. (*To* FATHER.) GET OUT OF MY WAY.

(FATHER *protects* MATILDA.)

She hates me, she wishes I was dead — DON'T YOU? Well I'm going to kill her and see how she likes it!

(*She dives at* MATILDA.)

FATHER   Hang on a minute woman, give the girl a chance to speak!

(MATILDA *says nothing.*)

MOTHER   RIGHT!

(*She takes another dive.*)

I want Mrs Crab reimbursed for that wreath.

FATHER   You can take it back.

MOTHER   No refunds on wreaths, so eleven pounds or I'll kill her!

FATHER   No refunds on wreaths! That's disgusting, I'll
            write to someone about that.

MOTHER   It's not the point, Frank!!

FATHER   Are you sure it was Matilda, the old woman
            might have got it wrong.

MOTHER   Of course it was Matilda, Mrs Crab was in the
            middle of telling half the street when I walked in
            the post office — brain tumour, apparently —
            very sudden!

FATHER   It's a lovely wreath though Mother, she obviously
            thought the world of you.

MOTHER   But I'm alive, Frank!

FATHER   Of course you are dear.

MOTHER   What will everybody say?

FATHER   (to MATILDA) You won't tell her?

MATILDA   No.

FATHER   You definitely won't tell her your mother's still
            alive?

MATILDA   No.

FATHER   (to MOTHER) Right then, we'll have to keep you
            locked in here and wear a lot of black.

MOTHER   Oh I'm glad you think it's funny — I'm really
            glad you find it funny that your daughter is a liar,
            your son's an emotional wreck, your neighbour's
            in a state of shock and your wife's the
            humiliation of the street!!

FATHER   What? What are you talking about?

MOTHER   You go out there, go on — hold your bloody head
            up if you can!

FATHER   Calm down love!

MOTHER   You're like a pair of children.

FATHER   She is a child!

MOTHER   She's seventeen Frank — seventeen!

FATHER   I don't know why you're getting so worked up.

MOTHER   Oh shut up Frank — shut your mouth.

          (*She slaps him sharply around the face.*)

FATHER   We seem to have upset your mother Matilda, and
          I'm being dead serious — oh come on love, try
          and see the joke.

MICHAEL   Its always the bloody same!! Me and my mother
          have got to see the joke!! It's not funny Dad. It's
          just not funny.

MOTHER   (*to* MATILDA) Can't you see how you upset me?

MATILDA   I don't care.

MICHAEL   Well don't care was MADE TO CARE,
          Don't care was hung
          Don't care was put in a pot and
          boiled till he was done!!!

MATILDA   (*sarcastically*) Was he really?

          (*She gets off the chair.*)

MOTHER   Where do you think you're going?

MATILDA   To my room!

          (*She storms into her bedroom. She can hear their
          voices raised.*)

MICHAEL   Oh let her go — she leaves a nasty smell in here
          anyway.

FATHER   Don't you talk about your sister like that.

MICHAEL   Why not? You know what she's like, why have
               you always got to side with her? Look how she
               upsets my mother . . .

FATHER   Because your mother gets upset at every little
               thing, I'm telling you, you've got to take it with a
               pinch of salt, she's a teenager, I was just the
               same at her age, playing pranks and getting
               myself into scrapes. It's not the end of the world.

               (*Thumping music has built up over the latter part
               of the scene. It continues through to* MATILDA'S
               room where she speaks aloud urgently.)

MATILDA   Dear Marjorie,
               You've got to get me out of here — my mother
               hates me, my dad's doin' my head in and my
               brother just sits there staring into space, I need
               the slimming tablets fast. I mean it Marjorie,
               you're my only hope — Matilda.

               (*Cut back to* FIONA'S *office. She swings out on
               swivel chair. She is on her mobile phone.*)

FIONA   Richard, hi — its me . . . Fiona. Listen Richard
               I'm going home for the weekend, so I need some
               information, on the kids, how old are they again?
               I know I've missed their birthdays, I've been
               really busy, so its five and three and Tommy's
               hair's changed colour — great — I'm fine, and
               how are you? Kiss them for me and next week's
               cheque is in the post. Bye.

               (*She hangs up and allows her tension to subside.*)

               I suppose I'd better tell you about Richard.

               (*She lights a cigarette and settles herself in
               chair.*)

               I know it'll sound stupid to you but I wanted the
               perfect man, I dreamed about him in every detail.
               He was dark, attractive with a small mole on his

left cheekbone. He would openly admire me and I
would secretly admire him and he would make me
feel special and sexy and strong. We would be
married in a huge church, Dad would give me
away and all the family would think I must be
really something to have won a man like that . . .
Then I met Richard. He had dark hair and a
freckle and his smile was ok so that was that,
being the nearest thing to the man I'd dreamed
of, I grabbed him with both hands. I started to
fantasise about our relationship, make up stories
with happy endings every time we had a fight,
because we did fight, all the time. I'd tell him
that I loved him and in my dreams he'd say 'I
love you too' but in fact all he ever said was "do
you?" or "so you say", as if he never really
believed me and maybe he was right, maybe I
didn't love him, but I tried to. I kept hoping one
day he'd just get out of bed, drag me up and help
me dress, take me on a surprise outing to a
country spot where he'd talk about my eyes and
compare them to the stars and he'd take me in his
arms and whisper that he wanted me, needed me
and he'd squeeze me so tight I'd think I would
die, then he'd pull me to a grassy bank and make
love to me like I was someone he'd always
dreamed of too. But I had to arrange the trips for
Richard 'cause he never wanted to go anywhere.
I'd push him and pull him and he'd reluctantly
comply, but he was tense and tired and more
often than not would fall asleep and be
unwakeable, he could sleep for hours with a little
smile on his face. I never knew what he dreamt
about but I guessed it wasn't me. And when he
was awake he'd sit in silence and ignore me or
drone on about things that I didn't even care
about let alone understand like ground frost and
plumbing and he'd repeat the same ideas to me
over and over again until I was numb to his
thoughts and closed to his feelings and that's the
only time he seemed to want me when I didn't
want him, and he'd paw at me and claw at me
and roll me over and fuck me like he wanted to
hurt me. He clearly worshipped the children, he

was very attentive, always picking them up, taking them out, talking to them. I never knew he could talk so much. When they cried in the night he would jump out of bed to comfort them, he was always awake these days, awake and in charge. He took over it felt like and elbowed me out, I never could have imagined how it would feel to be jealous of your own children, to feel worthless and useless because you'd done your job and were out of the picture, it wasn't how I'd dreamt it. But where dreams had once fooled me now they would save me, just the thought that maybe I could step out on my own began to excite me. I imagined getting a little place somewhere, furnished to my taste where I cooked the food I liked and ate the food I cooked. My place, my choice, my life. And once I'd imagined it, it happened, quite simply really. I went to night school, put down a deposit on a flat, told Richard I was divorcing him and left. He didn't even try and stop me. I've never told my family about my life because they wouldn't understand why I don't want my children. I don't want them, I'm sorry. My dad was so thrilled with Richard marrying his princess, and they say the western world doesn't have arranged marriages.

(*Lights out on* FIONA. *She exits. Lights rise on the dining room.* MICHAEL *is sitting at the table now set with party plates and hats. He clutches his fish tank which is now filled with water. He suddenly ducks his head into the tank, trying to drown himself.* MOTHER *enters and catches sight of him.*)

MOTHER   Michael, what are you doing? Son?

MICHAEL   (*lifting his face up*) Leave me alone will you?

          (MOTHER *has just about had enough.*)

MOTHER   There's some fish feed in the bathroom, I'll get it for you shall I?

(*She exits stage right as* MICHAEL *gets a chair. He stands on it, takes off his belt and hangs it from the ceiling light. He is trying to hang himself when* FATHER *enters carrying a stack of balloons.*)

FATHER   Help me pin these balloons up while you're up there son. Here come down, I'll start you off.

(MICHAEL *nearly kills himself falling off the chair.* FATHER *steps up on* MICHAEL'S *chair.*)

Here look, there's a belt up here — you can have that, son. (*He passes it to* MICHAEL.)

MICHAEL   Oh thanks.

(MOTHER *enters purposefully, carrying a large pin. She pops the balloons that* FATHER *is urgently hanging.*)

FATHER   Eh, what are you doing that for?

MOTHER   Because its ridiculous, Michael doesn't need reminding does he? He's trying to forget about Elain—

(MOTHER *cuts herself off but too late.* MICHAEL *is twitching,* FATHER *is twitching — she bites her tongue and exits.*)

MOTHER   Yes and I'll see if I can find those streamers.

FATHER   I think the red ones are best, don't you Michael? Michael?

(MICHAEL *makes a hasty exit with* FATHER *hot on his heels. He appears seconds later with an electric toaster which he is about to drop in the fish tank as* MATILDA *enters.*)

MATILDA   Michael, don't — Think of the fish!

(FATHER *enters.*)

FATHER	Is everybody happy!! It's all coming together, eh kids?
MATILDA	Michael, please come with me.
FATHER	I think Michael's going to help his Dad move the furniture, aren't you lad?
MICHAEL	Ok.
FATHER	You can start in the kitchen, Princess — your mother will show you what to do.
MATILDA	I can't. I've got to go.
FATHER	Go where?
MATILDA	I'm meeting someone.
FATHER	Who?
MATILDA	My prince.
FATHER	Not now Princess, we've got a party to organise!
MATILDA	But what about the wedding?
FATHER	What wedding?
MATILDA	My wedding — the one you're paying for!
FATHER	Yes, yes, all in good time Matilda, plenty of time.
MATILDA	But I haven't got time.
FATHER	Just get in the kitchen.
MATILDA	But I have to go now!
FATHER	Just do as you're told.
MATILDA	But you want me to meet him!
FATHER	Can't you be grateful for once in your selfish life instead of talking to me about princes! I don't

want you seeing princes! I want you here helping
me out — now get in the kitchen and start!

*(Music builds. "Adagio of Strings". She runs into
her bedroom, tears off her coat and stands before
the mirror. She is angry and upset, this time at
her FATHER.)*

MATILDA When I was a little girl my father was a king, a
king that spoke of princes and princesses. A king
that promised fairy-tale weddings and Cratchit
Christmas's, a king that was married to a queen
that someday I might mirror in a kingdom of my
own. I would fantasise about letting down my
hair 'til a canny prince climbed up it, I would
ponder over spinning wheels that pricked and
poisoned 'til I be awakened by a stranger's lips. I
lived in hope of rosy apples with lethal juices so
that I could die to be reborn by a handsome hunk
on horseback. And I listened to my king as he
whispered to his princess and I believed him and
I trusted him and I loved him and I wondered at
him with his strength and charm and wisdom and
I waited and I waited and so patiently I waited,
some day my prince will come, some day my
prince will come and he'll come, eventually but
driving a Ford Cortina, not on horseback, and
instead of waking me with his lips, he'll lash out
at me with his tongue and whenever I let down
my hair for him he'll pull at it 'til I scream, and
he will be dark — as had been promised, but the
darkness will be in his eyes and there will be no
fairy tale wedding and there will be no Cratchit
Christmas and he'll have lied to me my king, all
along he'll have lied, for when I asked him what
has happened to his promise, he will laugh and
say this is the real world and where I had once
believed I had seen his crown will sit a battered
trilby hat and his robe will be a mere overcoat
and the king will be a mere man, and when I
remember his queen whom I was meant to mirror,
I'll see a sad and ugly reflection of distorted
hopes and squashed dreams.

MOTHER   (*interrupting*) What are you doing?

MATILDA   Reading, so get out!!

MOTHER   There's a parcel come for you, special delivery.
            I've put it in the kitchen . . .

MATILDA   What is it?

            (*Without waiting for her reply she is gone to the
            kitchen.* MOTHER *sneaks inside.*)

MOTHER   (*putting books in sack*) Rapunzel,
            Rumpelstiltskin, Snow White, Red Rose, Beauty
            and the Beast, Sleeping Beauty, Cinderella, The
            Frog Prince, Little Red Riding Hood, good, good,
            good!

            (*She drags the sack into the sitting room where*
            FATHER *and* MICHAEL *are moving chairs ready for
            the party.*)

FATHER   What's that you've got, Mother?

            (*She stops dead in her tracks.*)

MOTHER   Oh, its just some old Christmas bunting I got
            down from the loft, I thought you might have
            wanted it.

FATHER   Yes, great, bring it here.

MOTHER   No, it's too tatty Frank. I'm throwing it out.

FATHER   Oh lets have a look.

MOTHER   It's no good Frank. Ok, it's shit!

FATHER   Alright, alright, there's no need for any of that!

            (*She drags it off stage as* MATILDA *enters and
            runs upstairs to her room clutching a package to
            her chest. She frantically rips open the package
            where she finds a letter and a smaller package.
            She reads the letter aloud.*)

MATILDA   Dear Matilda,

            Thank you for all your letters. I realise that you
            are in distress and if it is within my power to
            help you, then I will. Please find enclosed a little
            something to help with your dilemma. You'll find
            inside the package a sample potion in capsule
            form so it's nice and easy to swallow. The little
            pink pill is very potent and there is only one so a
            word of warning before you take it . . .

            (MATILDA *quickly rips open the small package
            and discovers the pill.*)

            (*whispering aloud*) Please make it work, please
            make me thin.

            (*She pops the pill and continues reading.*)

            . . . Once swallowed you will be compelled to tell
            the truth at all times and to everyone, including
            yourself. There is no turning back so be sure
            you're good and ready. I hope you'll find as I did
            that truth and not slimming pills will be your
            door to adulthood and freedom. Take care, I'll be
            thinking of you.

            Marjorie.

            (MATILDA *stands up. She is visibly shaken. She
            walks over to her mirror and looks into it.*)

MATILDA   Mirror, mirror, on the wall . . . what the fuck
            have I done?

            (*Thunder cracks. Lightening strikes. Matilda
            clutches a pair of scissors and stares at them as
            she opens and closes them several times. The
            lights fade down on this image.*)

FATHER   (*out of the darkness*) SURPRISE! ! ! ! !

ACT TWO

When the lights come up on the sitting room MOTHER, FATHER
and MICHAEL *are sitting around the table wearing their party
hats.* FIONA *has just walked through the door.*

FIONA   Hello Daddy, hello Mummy!

             (FATHER *giggles gleefully.*)

MOTHER   Frank — you have never dragged her here for
             this?

FIONA   I wouldn't have missed it for the world. How are
             you Michael?

MICHAEL   (*very tense*) Fine.

MOTHER   Where are the children?

FIONA   Tummy upsets, so Richard's had the day off
             work, but I'm here so . . .

             (*She gets a present out of her bag and hands it to*
             MICHAEL.)

             Happy anniversary, Michael and Elaine!

             (MICHAEL *starts to twitch,* MOTHER *starts to twitch,*
             FATHER *starts to twitch so* FIONA *starts to twitch,*
             quickly retracting the present and hiding it
             behind her back.)

             Where's Matilda?

MATILDA   I'm here.

             (MATILDA *is standing outside her bedroom door*
             with a strange look on her face. She has chopped
             off all her hair, although she seems to be as
             surprised by this as everyone else.)

MOTHER   Well, say hello to your sister.

MATILDA   Bollocks!

(MATILDA and family are all shocked.)

MOTHER   *(whispering)* What did she say?

MATILDA   I said Bollocks! Oops! Sorry . . . that's a horrible dress you're wearing Fiona.

(Everyone is shocked, including MATILDA.)

MOTHER   What's happened to your hair?

FATHER   Princess! Where have all your lovely locks gone?

MATILDA   No one can climb up it and no one can pull at it, it's mine now.

(She is as confused by this comment as everyone else.)

FATHER   Eh?

FIONA   I think it suits you.

MATILDA   Creep!

(MATILDA puts her hand over her mouth in surprise.)

FATHER   *(changing the subject)* How's Richard, still busy?

FIONA   He never stops.

FATHER   I hope he's finding time for you and those kids.

FIONA   Well he's busy Dad — he's successful.

FATHER   Bringing home plenty of bacon is he?

FIONA   Yes.

FATHER   Do you hear that Mother? Brilliant isn't it?

MOTHER   Well its nice to know somebody's achieving, Frank.

(MATILDA *has made her way downstairs to join
the family. They all have one eye on her.*)

FATHER   That's what I said, it's brilliant! Now then girls
            what about your party hats? Here you are Matilda,
            cover up that haircut.

MATILDA   I don't want to wear a stupid hat!

MOTHER   Matilda!

FATHER   It's alright love, she's only joking.

            (MATILDA *is almost gagging trying not to let her
            response escape.*)

FIONA   I'll have mine Daddy,

FATHER   Here you are Tillie, put yours on.

MATILDA   (*bursts out*) Fuck off! Oh God, I'm sorry.

            (*The family are absolutely horrified.* MOTHER
            bangs her fists on the table.)

MOTHER   Don't you DARE use that language to your father!

FATHER   I don't think she said what you think she said
            Mother — did you Tillie? We must have all
            misheard her, now sit down like a good girl and
            we'll say no more about it. Now, whose for some
            of your mother's chocolate cake?

MATILDA   Please Dad no . . . please don't make us!

FATHER   It's your favourite Matilda.

            (MATILDA *starts to heave visibly, they all try and
            ignore it.*)

            You'll have some won't you Fiona?

FIONA   Mmm, lovely.

            (*He franticaly cuts* FIONA *a large slice.*)

FATHER   Michael?

MICHAEL   Go on then.

(MATILDA *is heaving and retching, making the most horrible sounds.*)

FATHER   Mother, fancy a slice?

MOTHER   No thank you.

FATHER   Come on then Tillie, eat or leave the table please.

(MATILDA *vomits onto her plate. The family's reaction is one of undisguised repulsion.*)

ALL   Ohhh . . . oh no! Oh dear! . . . disgusting, etc.

FATHER   What on earth's the matter with you Matilda? Why didn't you say you weren't well?

MATILDA   Please don't ask me Dad, don't ask me to explain.

FATHER   Its alright Princess, you can't help being poorly, Mother — clear up the mess will you?

MOTHER   Oh thanks very much.

FATHER   Now come on and tell your old Dad what made you sick. I thought you loved Mum's chocolate cake.

MATILDA   I only ever ate it to please you — you wanted me to like it, but its made me sick ever since . . .

FATHER   Ever since what Tillie?

MATILDA   Nooo! I . . . it . . . ever since one birthday when I was little and I took a bite of chocolate cake with a hair entwined in the middle, it gagged in my throat and I thought I was going to choke to death so I ran upstairs to find you but you were wanking in the bedroom and the first sighting of your willy with cake stuck in my throat just caused a phobic reaction!

(*She is exhausted by the burst of speech and obviously embarrassed. The family are stunned.* FATHER *starts to twitch.* MOTHER *stares at him in disgust.*)

MOTHER   I think you'd better go to bed.

MATILDA   But Dad wants us all to be together.

FATHER   No, go to your room, you're obviously not feeling well.

MATILDA   But I feel better now honestly, like a giant weight has been lifted off my shoulders.

MOTHER   Get to bed Matilda!

FATHER   Now let's just try and start this again, with a drink! Here we are Michael . . .

MICHAEL   No thank you.

FATHER   Come on Michael have a drink, a drink with your family.

MICHAEL   I don't want one.

FIONA   Have a drink Michael.

FATHER   Of course he'll have a drink.

MICHAEL   I just don't feel like one, ok?

FATHER   You'll have a drink with your family Michael, this is a party, everyone must drink at a party or it's not a real party, isn't that right Fiona?

FIONA   Of course its not a real party unless you have a drink, Michael.

MOTHER   You'd better have a small one Michael.

MICHAEL   I don't want one!!

FATHER   But you're spoiling the party atmosphere son, help me out here, let go of the glass.

FIONA   Don't be a spoil-sport, let Dad pour your drink.

FATHER   What's the matter with you, son? Hold the glass still, there you go, now drink it.

(FATHER *has lost his temper and spilt wine all over* MICHAEL. MICHAEL *takes a swig whilst all eyes are on him. As they look away he spits it back into his glass.*)

MATILDA   He just spat it back into his glass. Oh sorry Michael.

(MICHAEL *glares at* MATILDA.)

FATHER   Of course he didn't spit it back into his glass — did you son?

MICHAEL   No.

FIONA   Still telling lies, Matilda?

MATILDA   Still wetting the bed, Fiona? (MATILDA *cringes,* FIONA *glares.*) God, I'm gasping for a fag. Tut!

(*She is irritated that she has no control over her truths.*)

FATHER   You don't smoke.

MATILDA   Yes I do, I have done since I was twelve . . . damn.

FATHER   Well, don't.

MATILDA   Have you got a cigarette, Fiona?

FIONA   (*defensively*) I don't smoke!

MATILDA   Well you used to — you gave me my first one.

FIONA   She's lying Dad, I never did!

FATHER   Of course you didn't, you've always been
            responsible.

MATILDA   Big tits.

FIONA   What did she say?

MATILDA   I'm sorry — I didn't mean to say it. I was just
            thinking what big tits you have.

MOTHER   Don't be so rude Matilda.

MATILDA   I'm really sorry, it just popped out.

MOTHER   Well try keeping your mouth shut.

            (*She sits there trying even harder to keep her lips
            together.*)

FATHER   Would anybody like any ice cream and jelly?

MATILDA   I'd like to have jelly spread all over me . . .

            (*She positively rams her fist in her mouth to stop
            the words coming out.*)

MOTHER   You're giving me a headache.

FATHER   Yes, go to bed if you can't behave!

MATILDA   You never behave yourself . . .

FATHER   I don't have to — I'm an adult.

MATILDA   You've got a silly hat on, you get excited at
            cartoons, you read my fairy tales, if anyone
            should behave it's you! . . . (*She looks
            apologetic.*)

FATHER   But I already am behaving!

MATILDA   No you're not.

FATHER   And how would you have me behave?

MATILDA   As yourself, the self you never show, the self you
            disguise with party hats and crackers!

FATHER   Where have you got these daft ideas from? Have
              you been talking to your mother? (*To* MOTHER.)
              Have you been talking to Matilda? Ha, ha, ha, I
              don't know. Anyway I need the toilet . . . excuse me.

MATILDA   Come back Dad . . .

              (MICHAEL *is sitting with his head bowed.* MOTHER
              and FIONA *look very tense.*)

MOTHER   (*changing the subject*) So Fiona, how is Richard?

MATILDA   Yes Fiona, how is Richard?

FIONA   (*angry*) Oh he's fine, doing brilliantly at work.

MATILDA   DON'T IGNORE ME!

FIONA   I think I'll go and phone him actually, check the
              kids are alright.

MOTHER   I'll come with you, have a word with them.

FIONA   No, they'll be asleep. You stay here with Matilda.

              (FIONA *exits.*)

MATILDA   Mum wants to speak to her grandchildren and
              you won't let her!

MOTHER   I don't want to speak to them — mind your own
              business. Come on Michael, let's go and find
              your father. Bring that bottle, will you?

              (MOTHER *carries out paper plates and cups, while*
              MICHAEL *tentatively approaches the table to pick
              up remaining bottle.* MATILDA *is alone at the
              table — muttering as if possessed.*)

MATILDA   You're leaving me on my own, I don't like being
              on my own, I'm always on my own, you always
              leave me on my own and I don't like being on my
              own. Bastards . . . don't leave me . . .

(The family have congregated in the kitchen, huddled together in a spotlight. They peer towards MATILDA.)

FATHER   You know you don't want to take any notice of her tales, it seems to me that mentally she's going off the rails.

MOTHER   For God's sake Frank this is all your fault, she gets more malicious every day.

FATHER   Well if you'd have given her a bit more freedom she probably wouldn't be this way.

MOTHER   You can't blame me for keeping her in, not after everything she's said and done!

MICHAEL We keep telling you what a liar she is.

FATHER   I see what you mean this time my son, that nasty tale she told about me was enough to put me off my tea. *(To* FIONA.*)* And as for saying you look a mess, I've never seen such a lovely dress, but she's still your sister, she's still our child.

FIONA   She's turning absolutely wild, look at the way she's sitting there, grinning and pulling at her hair!

FATHER   I can't think what's got into her, she must have had too much to drink.

FIONA   Oh cheer up Daddy, it's still a party, dancing or party games, what do you think?

MOTHER   Yes, try and ignore her, leave her be, enjoy our celebration tea.

FATHER   Get the Trivial Pursuit from off the shelf and maybe she'll behave herself . . .

(They troop round into the dining area carrying a box of Trivial Pursuit. MATILDA looks up.)

MOTHER   Here it is.

FATHER   Right then, here we go, what colour do you want
              to want to be, Michael?

MICHAEL   I don't care.

FATHER   Pink then.

MICHAEL   Not pink.

FATHER   Alright, yellow then.

FIONA   I'll be pink.

MOTHER   And I'll have blue.

FATHER   I'll be green — right here we go!

MATILDA   What about me?

FIONA   You're not playing.

MOTHER   You're not very well.

FATHER   Why don't you sit quietly and have a rest, I don't
              think too much excitement is good for you.

MATILDA   You don't want me to play do you?

FATHER   (*looking at others hopelessly*) Of course we want
              you to play Matilda, you can be orange . . .
              alright I'll start.

              (*He throws the dice enthusiastically.*)

FATHER   Six! Ha! Ha! Six! Six! Six!

FIONA   Oh you're so clever Dad, what colour question?

FATHER   I'll have pink for entertainment please.

FIONA   What actress starred with Gene Kelly in "Singing
              in the Rain"?

FATHER   Easy, peasy — Debbie Reynolds.

FIONA   Yes.

FATHER   Hurray! Hurray! I get a little hat.

FIONA   Well done, Dad.

           (*He throws the dice and it rolls under the table.*)

FATHER   Oh yes! It's another six, ha ha.

MATILDA   It wasn't a six, it was a two.

FIONA   Another pink question?

FATHER   Yes please.

MATILDA   He can't just choose a colour, he has to have the
           one he's landed on.

MOTHER   Not now, Matilda.

MATILDA   But he's cheating!

FIONA   Who starred with Dustin Hoffman in "All the
           President's Men"?

FATHER   Eh . . . Robert De Niro?

FIONA   Correct.

MATILDA   It was Robert Redford, it was definitely Robert
           Redford.

MOTHER   And Robert De Niro.

MATILDA   Liar.

MOTHER   Don't you call me a liar, you're the only liar in
           this house. Throw the dice, Frank.

MATILDA   You're going to let him win aren't you? You're
           all just going to sit there and let him win, the big
           baby . . . oh!

FATHER   What's the matter Princess, don't you want your
           old Dad to win?

MATILDA   Cheat!

FATHER   It's that haircut, it's gone to her head.

FIONA   Yes, stop telling lies Matilda.

MATILDA   Oh help me, please . . . I don't like this . . . I
           don't like it, I don't like it, I DON'T LIKE IT!

           (*Her tongue running away with her is causing her
           much distress.*)

FATHER   I think she's upset — I think we're being too
           hard on her . . .

           (*The others are annoyed. She has her hand over
           her mouth again.*)

           Now you can choose the next game, what would
           you like to play? Pass the parcel?

           (*She nods.*)

           Ok then . . . you go into the kitchen and make up
           a parcel while I organise the music. Shall we
           have our favourite house LP on?

MATILDA   It's my favourite house LP, you old fool. Shit!

           (*She runs out.*)

FATHER   (*to others*) She's probably only joking.

           (*Blackout. 'House' music fills the stage. When
           the lights come up the family are sitting cross-
           legged, except for MATILDA. FATHER has the
           parcel and he is moving to the music, unwilling
           to let go of it. He offers it to MICHAEL then
           snatches it away again. The family are getting
           increasingly annoyed with him. She demands he
           pass it around. MATILDA stops the music as it
           lands on MOTHER. MOTHER reluctantly opens the
           box and there is a question written on the lid.*)

MOTHER   What's this?

MATILDA   It's a question and whatever it asks you must
               answer truthfully — I'm not doing this on my
               own.

MOTHER   I'm not answering that, Matilda.

FATHER   What does it say?

MATILDA   "Have you ever masturbated?"

FATHER   For God's sake Matilda, what kind of a game is
               this?

MATILDA   Mother, you must answer truthfully.

               (*All are embarrassed, except* MOTHER *who has
               had enough and shouts.*)

MOTHER   Yes! . . . Yes, yes, yes!

               (FIONA *screams and giggles until she sees the
               look on* FATHER'S *face.*)

FATHER   When?

MOTHER   For God's sake Frank, I've answered the
               question. I don't think we need a public debate!

MATILDA   Very good . . . five points!

               (*She puts music on and although* MOTHER *looks
               quite proud of herself they all pass the parcel
               furiously as no one wants to answer another
               question — when the music stops.*)

FATHER   Hey — that's not fair. It stopped on you Michael,
               you threw it back.

MICHAEL   No I didn't, you hadn't passed it to me.

FATHER   Michael take the parcel, don't cheat.

MICHAEL   I'm not cheating, its you!

(FIONA *snatches the box off* FATHER, *opens the lid and reads.*)

FIONA   Dad, "how often do you change your underwear? Every day, every week or every month?"

FATHER   Every day.

MOTHER   Lies, lies, lies, every two weeks he changes his pants, its disgusting.

FATHER   I should know how often I change my own knickers!

MOTHER   I know because I wash them!

MATILDA   Right then Dad, you have to perform a forfeit. You must kiss Michael and tell him you love him.

FATHER   Alright, I only change my underpants every two weeks, what's the big deal in that?

MOTHER   Yes, don't be silly Matilda, its only a game.

FATHER   I thought we'd be playing sensible games.

MATILDA   (*snaps*) Well telling the truth is sensible, isn't it? I thought you were a Christian.

FATHER   Don't bring religion into pass the parcel, Matilda. It isn't right.

             (*She puts the music back on, they pass the parcel and it lands on* FATHER *again. He unwraps and reads.*)

             "What is your biggest fear"? Playing this game for the rest of my life, there you are and that's the truth now move on.

             (*She continues the music. The family behave as though the parcel were a bomb. Eventually it lands on* FIONA.)

FIONA Shit . . . I mean damn, Daddy.

     (*She unwraps it and reads.*)

     How many men have you slept with?

MATILDA There's been a mistake, that one isn't for you. It's for Michael!

     (*She immediately regrets the words.* MICHAEL *glares at her and then gets to his feet and chases her out of sight. Lights fade down on the scene as music plays. When the lights rise,* MATILDA *is hiding behind the staircase. The family are dispersed across the stage. All of them are purposeful and dangerously angry.*)

FATHER I think we've got to face the fact that much as it makes me very sad, the party's over 'cause Matilda's gone absolutely raving mad.

MICHAEL I think Dad's right, it's serious, we should get a doctor round here fast, he'll section her with any luck, she could be locked up by quarter past.

FIONA She's just a heartless brutal cow, trying to destroy this family's calm.

MICHAEL She's doing it deliberately to cause us individual harm.

MOTHER She's done enough to you my son, I wish I'd killed her, I should have done, your father should have made her pay for wrecking your only wedding day.

FATHER I should have belted her for that but I didn't know she was such a brat, I thought it was a joke you see.

MICHAEL Well it was a joke — with the laugh on me!

FATHER She ruined that day for me and your mother.

MOTHER She's always been jealous of her brother.

FIONA   Well whatever you decide to do, give me a ring
         and let me know, there's not much point in my
         being here, I've kids at home, I should really go.

FATHER   Don't leave us with her Fiona love, we need you
         here to lend support.

FIONA   Well what do you want me to do!!?

MICHAEL Take her with you.

         (FIONA *looks horrified.*)

         It was just a thought.

         (FATHER *picks up the cruise brochures. He flicks
         through them.*)

FATHER   A family cruise what a great idea, we could sail
         tonight and leave her here.

         (MATILDA *enters. They all jump at her sudden
         entrance.*)

         Hello Matilda darling . . . I was only joking about
         not taking you.

MATILDA You've no intention of going on a family cruise,
         not tonight, not ever.

MOTHER   Shut up Matilda.

MATILDA You've kept my mother drooling at the mouth
         with your promises and your dreams.

MOTHER   Stop it Matilda!

MATILDA You promised her a white wedding then put her
         in a tweed twin suit and roughed it down the
         registry office. You promised her a honeymoon,
         then a second honeymoon, then a third and a
         fourth, always somewhere exotic, out of reach,
         but she always ended up in Blackpool. You've let
         her waste her life on your crummy dreams and

it's not easy to overcome the let down and disappointment and confusion when you're promised something every day and I wouldn't go on a cruise ship with you if you paid me because you know something Dad? You'd promise us that we'd be coming home again as we find ourselves marooned on some shitty little island because you could only afford the one-way ticket but didn't want to tell us!

(FATHER'S *mouth is trembling.* MATILDA *is shocked at her own outburst.*)

I'm sorry, I don't know where that came from, it just came out.

(*She moves to her* FATHER.)

Sorry Dad.

(*He pushes her away. She runs off upset into her bedroom.* MOTHER *runs after her, in a rage.*)

MOTHER   What the hell do you think you're playing at? Upsetting your father like that!

MATILDA   You don't love him — you've never loved him! (*She gasps, shocked at the words.*)

MOTHER   Is that your honest opinion?

MATILDA   Yes . . .

MOTHER   Well so what?

MATILDA   What do you mean, so what?

MOTHER   So what if I don't love him, what's it to you?

MATILDA   What's it to me? What about Dad?

MOTHER   This is real life Matilda, how long do you think we'd have lasted if we'd been honest with each other? Five minutes instead of twenty five years? You learn a lot about people in twenty five years, you learn to negotiate, compromise, live together, raise kids together, shut him up when he goes too far, comfort him when he's in distress, you learn that even if you don't love him, you sometimes like him, you certainly need him and what's more you want him anyway because he's better than nothing — and we tell each other it's love but I know damn well it's not and if the real thing ever came along I'd take it like a shot but it hasn't and it won't and so I stay. I stay where I am because it's where I want to be, safe, secure and warm — you can save your love for the homeless Matilda, they're cold and hungry and need it more than me!!!

MATILDA   Everyone needs love.

MOTHER   Oh grow up, Goldilocks!

MATILDA   I can hear you having sex from my bedroom, but they're hollow and empty, your moans.

(MOTHER'S *mouth drops open.*)

When I get a lover I'll tell him what I want — lick me, suck me, touch me, fuck me, stroke me, push me, pull me, whip me!

MOTHER   What a liar you are Matilda, no woman would want to behave like that.

MATILDA   It is you who's telling lies, I can see that in your eyes.

(MOTHER *storms out of* MATILDA'S *room to join the others.* MATILDA, *who can't believe what she just said to her* MOTHER, *studies herself in the mirror.*)

MATILDA   Matilda, stop it, what are you saying??!

(*Meanwhile, in the sitting room.*)

MOTHER   I'm not sure what she's playing at, but whatever it is I've had enough, she's out for vengeance that's for sure.

MICHAEL   I think its time we played it rough!

FATHER   Well we're going to have to keep an eye on what she's planning for her next trick.

FIONA   I'm frightened Daddy, don't let her hurt us.

FATHER   I'll protect you, let's get her quick!

MOTHER   I have to warn you she's over sexed, I don't know what she'll come out with next.

FATHER   More fables, tales and vicious lies, I'll have to knock her down to size. Now remember everybody I'm the leader, lets crucify the little bleeder!

             (*They all scuttle behind* FATHER *up the staircase to* MATILDA'S *room. They hover one on each step, listening in.* MATILDA *is talking to herself in the mirror.*)

MATILDA   Mirror, mirror, on the wall, who is the ugliest of them all? You are Matilda, you are the ugliest of them all. You are ugly and disgusting and repulsive and a disgrace and they hate you Matilda — do you hear me? They hate you!

             (*Outside her door, the family whisper.*)

FIONA   What's she doing in there?

FATHER   Ranting and raving like a mad thing. Sssh . . .

             (*They continue listening nervously.*)

MATILDA   But you should not be afraid Matilda, they fear you but you need no longer fear them, so make way, make way for Matilda, go, go, go!

             (*The family flee in terror but nobody seems to be in charge.*)

MICHAEL   What are we doing?!!

FIONA I don't know — just HIDE!

(They all hide behind the table — FATHER *hides behind sofa.* MATILDA, *angry and upset, has rushed down to join them.)*

MATILDA Where is everybody? I know you're here, Dad. I can see you hiding behind the sofa, stand up, show yourself.

*(*FATHER *stands.)*

FATHER No Matilda, I wasn't hiding, I was just picking up some crumbs off the carpet.

MATILDA Booooo!!!

(She pounces at him, he jumps out of his skin.)

You see, you're frightened of me!

FATHER Frightened of you? Don't be silly, why would I be frightened of my own daughter?

MATILDA Because you're a coward and a liar and I can see where you dare not look — right through you! Come on the rest of you cowering in the corner — it's not me you fear, it's yourselves!

FATHER Look Matilda, we just want you back to your old self.

MATILDA There is no going back, I've found my voice and now you must listen.

(Music — Gershwin's "Rhapsody in Blue". MATILDA *runs up the spiral staircase as her family slowly rise and join* FATHER *in the middle of the room. As* MATILDA *begins her story, the family react as if under a spell, forced into action against their will. They stay very close but through the story move like a giant Sphinx.)*

Once upon a time there was a kingdom and in it lived a king and his family. The king would pass

out crowns to family members and give them
names: mother would be queen, boychild would
be prince, girlchildren princesses. The king was a
very friendly ruler who knew that to control his
subjects he needed an iron fist and a sharp
tongue, but the king did not possess these
qualities, so for fear of losing his crown he
instructed his family on how best to serve him.
The queen and his children would always be
happy, ask no questions and believe everything he
said. The queen and her children, knowing that
kings are always right, assumed their roles as
best they could.

(*Spotlight hits* MOTHER.)

MOTHER   (*trying hard, but losing it*) Yes dear, you look
very distinguished in your crown. Yes children,
of course I'll take you to the bus stop, yes I'll
have your shirts washed and your dresses ironed,
yes I'll cook the tea, yes I'm happy, yes you're
wonderful, yes I love you, yes I'll stay in while
you go out, yes I'll ease your pain, yes I'll always
be here, yes, yes, yes!

MATILDA   But it didn't take a fool to look at her and know,
when a woman says yes — she often means no.
For the queen dreamed of running away, escaping
the clutches of her family.

MOTHER   I feel desperately trapped, I cannot breathe for
the ties that bind me are getting tighter and
tighter, squeezing round my neck. My children
should be married off, I'm sick of being a mother.
They should let me run whilst they stand still,
I've done my bit, I've earned my freedom, but my
children stay, they stay and they stay, they
smother me, strangle me, torment me with their
presence and with every passing day they take
away my hope and bang the lid down on my
coffin.

MATILDA   And so the kingdom became like a huge jail to
her from which she would never break free.

Meanwhile in the castle, the young prince was in distress, ever since he was a child he had longed to be a queen. He knew it was preposterous for his father had named him prince and it was his job in life to one day be a king. He had met a girl in the neighbouring kingdom called Princess Elaine, who dreamed of a band of gold wrapped around her finger, his mother and father were overjoyed, a wedding in the kingdom! Meanwhile, Princess Matilda who was NOT chosen to be a bridesmaid, went tip-toe to her brother's room the night before the wedding and spied him with Elaine's brother Prince Stuart, who was meant for PRINCESS MATILDA NOT MICHAEL! She should have fled and ignored the sight but she was mesmerised by her brother's touch, she had ne'er seen this side to him for he had been a sullen child. It was next day at the wedding that Princess Fiona arrived. She had escaped the tower years before but the king and queen always overlooked this fact and welcomed her back with open arms, though why they bothered I'll never know for no sooner had Matilda opened her gob that Fiona wanted to go again!

(FIONA *begins to run around with angry sounds.* MICHAEL *joins her with fearful moans,* FATHER *joins them with cries of pain,* MOTHER *with sounds of rage.* MATILDA *dances in triumph from her tower showing them their true selves. When the sounds have built to a crescendo, at once they all break from the spell and the lights snap out and music cuts. There is a moment of quiet shock.*)

FATHER   What's this? Is there truth in what she's saying?

MOTHER   No, no of course not. She's distorting everything, telling lies.

FATHER   You feel trapped with me, you're plotting to leave?

MOTHER   I've just told you Frank, she's lying.

FATHER   (*to* MICHAEL) And you? What does she mean, a
           queen?

MICHAEL   (*frightened*) I don't know.

MATILDA   Yes you do know, Michael . . . tell them . . .

FATHER   Tell us what?

MATILDA   I shouted you were gay at the alter because I saw
           you kissing that boy.

MOTHER   What boy?

MICHAEL   It's a lie.

FATHER   Did you kiss a boy Michael? Did you? Did you?

MICHAEL   I hate you Matilda!

FATHER   Did you?

MICHAEL   No.

FATHER   Kissing boys is disgusting, kissing boys is
           unnatural, kissing boys is not what I brought you
           up to do!!

MICHAEL   I didn't do it, I love Elaine.

FATHER   Love Elaine? I'd like to rip the lips off your face.

MICHAEL   Why won't you believe me?

FATHER   Look at you — you did it — I can see you did it.

MOTHER   So what if he did? It was an innocent kiss, boys
           play such games before their weddings.

FATHER   I didn't!

MOTHER   No, but you slept with me when I didn't want you
           to, you forced yourself on me instead of waiting
           for my wedding night!

FATHER   What the hell has that got to do with him being a
           fairy!?

MOTHER   I'm just saying — we all make mistakes!

MICHAEL   But everyone knows she's a liar, everyone knows
          she tells lies just like she did about you and the
          chocolate cake!

          (FATHER *suddenly leaps on* MICHAEL. MICHAEL *tries
          to escape as* FATHER *continuously beats him up.
          The rest of the family are horrified.* MATILDA
          intervenes and with all her strength she drags
          FATHER *off* MICHAEL *and attacks him in a rage.*)

MATILDA   I hate you sometimes, I've hated you so much
          I've imagined you having a heart attack, I've
          imagined getting a knife and surprising you with
          it in the back, I've imagined whacking your head
          against a brick wall, *smack,* and blood pouring
          out of your eyes. I've wanted to see you shocked,
          in pain, on your knees, begging for forgiveness,
          then I'd punch you in the face and crack you with
          a stick and slice your belly down the middle and
          rip out your organs and shake you 'til your teeth
          rattled!!

MOTHER   Matilda!!

FIONA   (*panicking*) Mother, get her out of here quickly!

MATILDA   I'm sorry . . . I'm sorry . . .

MOTHER   Get to your room!

          (*She goes, looking shaken.* MICHAEL, *who is still
          huddled on the floor after his beating, follows*
          MATILDA *with his eyes.*)

MICHAEL   (*to* MATILDA) Happy now?

MOTHER   Michael, go and find something to do — go on —
          get out of here!

MICHAEL   What?

MOTHER   Go on — just go!

MICHAEL   Fine.

           (*He goes.*)

MOTHER   Fiona go and phone Richard, ask him to come
           will you?

FIONA   No Mum, I'm going home.

           (FATHER *who is standing in the middle of the
           room, looks up bewildered.*)

FATHER   Don't go Fiona, I haven't seen you . . .

FIONA   But I have to Dad, I mean, look at the time!

FATHER   What about our tea? We haven't finished our tea.

MOTHER   Come on Frank, sit down.

FATHER   We must finish our tea . . . it's a party . . .

MOTHER   Just sit down!!

           (MOTHER *jerks* FIONA *into the kitchen. She is
           quietly hysterical.*)

MOTHER   I think you'd better get Richard down here, your
           dad needs another man to talk to.

FIONA   He can't come Mum, he's busy.

MOTHER   He's always busy, can't he make one social trip
           for a family crisis?

FIONA   He won't.

MOTHER   What do you mean won't? What sort of a husband
           is he?

FIONA   An ex-husband.

MOTHER   What?

FIONA   He's gone.

MOTHER   What do you mean gone?

FIONA   He's gone — left me — for another woman . . .

MOTHER   Fiona stop it, don't!

FIONA   I wanted to tell you.

MOTHER   Well where are the kids?

FIONA   He snatched them.

MOTHER   What do you mean!

FIONA   He snatched them from their nursery.

MOTHER   Well tell him to give them back!!

FIONA   I tried Mum, but he wants them and well — he's got more money and everything — look, I can't tell you any more, you won't understand.

MOTHER   You have to tell me more Fiona, I have to know!

FIONA   It's over, that's all. I don't want to talk about it.

MOTHER   That's it? That's all I get? Can't anybody talk to me?

FIONA   Well you've made it hard, that's all — both of you.

MOTHER   I've given my life to you — your father worships the ground you walk on!

FIONA   Mum can we leave it?

MOTHER   No we cannot leave it! I won't leave it!

FIONA   Oh Mother, for God's sake — I never see my children — ever! They're ugly and stupid and cry whenever I go near them. I'm not like you — I've got a life. You made your choice — you married the silly bastard, you got exactly what you wanted.

MOTHER   How would you know what I wanted? How would you know that? What I gave up for you?

FIONA   (*angry now*) Oh what!!? What did you give up for
           me? A fantastic career? Another love? You have
           sacrificed nothing — so stop fantasising!

MOTHER   I thought I had to have children! I THOUGHT
           THEY WERE COMPULSORY!! I never wanted
           you, any of you!!!

           (FIONA *slaps her* MOTHER *across the face.*)

FIONA   I think that's a terrible thing to say.

MOTHER   I'm sorry Fiona . . . forgive me. I don't feel too
           well. I'll make a cup of tea. Will you go and see
           if your dad wants one for me . . . there's a good
           girl.

           (MOTHER *exits trembling.* FIONA *moves over to her*
           FATHER.)

FIONA   Do you want a cup of tea, Dad?

           (*He doesn't reply.*)

           Matilda tells lies Dad, she can't help it, don't let
           her get to you.

           (FIONA *moves across to* MICHAEL, *who has just
           entered.*)

           Why did you have to upset Dad? Couldn't you
           just deny it?

MICHAEL   I did deny it — I do deny it!

FIONA   Not to me, to him! I don't care what you are, but
           it'll kill Dad — you know it will.

MICHAEL   I don't know what to do.

FIONA   Go and convince him, he looks terrible.

MICHAEL   Come with me.

FIONA   No, you've got to sort it out. You might have
           been more careful Michael — more discreet!

MICHAEL   I feel sick.

FIONA   Go and get Matilda to say she lied.

MICHAEL   She won't.

FIONA   Well try, idiot!

(MICHAEL *makes his way towards the staircase as* MOTHER *crosses him on her way to* FIONA. *Light shifts up to* MATILDA'S *room where* MICHAEL *enters.*)

MATILDA   I love you Michael.

MICHAEL   I hate you Matilda. Go and tell him it was all a mistake.

MATILDA   I can't — go and tell him you love him.

MICHAEL   I can't.

MATILDA   I'll come with you.

MICHAEL   No — I'll never forgive you for this Matilda — never!

MATILDA   Forgive yourself.

MICHAEL   For what?

MATILDA   For being you, for hating me, for letting Mother hate me so she wouldn't hate you!

MICHAEL   How dare you? HOW DARE YOU blurt out my secrets on my wedding day. Have you never heard of timing?! Did you never think of tact?! What qualifications do you have to be chief advisor on my life? Huh?! Whatever I've done, however I've behaved it was MY choice and now you've wrecked it just like that because you're too bloody selfish to see behind my lies and respect my choice to tell them! I WANT A NORMAL LIFE!!!

MATILDA   How can denying who you are mean a normal
            life?

MICHAEL   BECAUSE LOVING YOUR PARENTS IS
            NORMAL, MATILDA. Only you're NOT
            NORMAL so you wouldn't know that!!!

            (*He leaves her as she turns to her mirror and
            spies the monster within.* MICHAEL *sneaks past his*
            FATHER *on the way to the kitchen where* FIONA *and*
            MOTHER *are talking.*)

FIONA   (*irritable*) We can't just sit here when Dad's so
            upset — can't you go and talk to him?

MOTHER   Fiona, did you know Michael was gay?

FIONA   Oh for God's sake Mother, he's not gay, ok? Just
            pretend she never said it.

MICHAEL   (*appearing*) I think Dad's having a funny turn.

            (*The three of them shuffle together to peek at
            him.*)

            He's shaking.

FIONA   He's gone a very funny colour.

MOTHER   Should I call a doctor?

FIONA   This is all Matilda's fault — give me that tea.

            (*She storms out with* MOTHER *and* MICHAEL *in
            tow.*)

            Here you are Daddy, a nice cup of tea.

            (FATHER *doesn't acknowledge them.* MATILDA
            comes out of her room.)

MATILDA   Why are you hovering around him? Is he ill?

FIONA   Of course he's ill, you've made him ill.

            (FATHER *suddenly stands to face* MATILDA.)

FATHER   Matilda, do you love me?

MATILDA   Yes Daddy, I love you.

FATHER   Then make all the nasty stories go away. Where's the love my little girl used to give me? Where's my little girl?

MATILDA   IT'S NO GOOD ASKING FOR YOUR LITTLE GIRL — I'M NOT A LITTLE GIRL I'M A MONSTER!

FATHER   I am telling you to stop it, I am your father, you do as I say!

MATILDA   YOU CANNOT STOP ME — I CANNOT BE STOPPED!

FATHER   Do you want a good hiding is that it?

MATILDA   YES, HIT ME! COME ON, HIT ME!

FATHER   (*clutching at straws*) Maybe some money? How much do you want? Five? Ten? One hundred and fifty?

MATILDA   Help me Daddy, please!

FATHER   Now pull yourself together!

MATILDA   FUCKING FAT BASTARD!

FATHER   Matilda look, look at me, I'm on my knees!

MATILDA   FUCKING FAT BASTARD!

FATHER   What can I do? Tell me what to do!

MATILDA   Just go Dad — YOU UGLY PIG!

(FIONA *has dragged* MICHAEL *up the stairs where they kick* MATILDA *into her bedroom whilst* MOTHER *helps* FATHER *crawl helplessly back to the table.* FIONA *locks* MATILDA *in a neck brace,* MICHAEL *holds her arm behind her back.*)

FIONA   Listen, if you don't stop all this I'm going to
             smash your little head in and get your fingernails
             and rip them off one by one — do you hear me?

MATILDA   I'm not frightened of you!

FIONA   Oh aren't you? Well you ought to be — don't you
             care who you upset?

MICHAEL   Yeah, "Don't Care" was made to care.

MATILDA   Like you've been made to care, Michael?

FIONA   Oh shut up! (*She shoves her away.*) Look, if you
             go and say you're sorry I'll give you those
             diamante earrings you've always liked, you can
             have them ok? They're yours.

MATILDA   I only pretended to like them Fiona, they're
             horrible!

FIONA   Well is there anything you do like? I'll give you
             anything you want.

MATILDA   Don't you understand I took a truth drug — I
             can't stop — I can't!

MICHAEL   There's no such thing as a truth drug.

MATILDA   There is and I took it and now I wish I hadn't but
             you can't stop me — I'm compelled!

FIONA   (*menacingly*) Oh, don't worry Matilda, we'll stop
             you alright.

MATILDA   DO YOUR WORST, BLOW YOUR PIPE UNTIL
             YOU BURST!

FIONA   Come on Michael!

MICHAEL   Wait . . . Matilda, did you break that vase when
             we were little, the one I got the blame for? The

one I had to pay for out of my pocket money for two years?

MATILDA   Yes!

MICHAEL   I knew it was you! I knew it. I knew it was her!

FIONA   Come on!

(*They return to the table having given* MATILDA *a kick for good measure.* MOTHER *is standing, fists clenched, seething.* FATHER *is sitting pathetically in a chair.*)

MOTHER   Truth drug my arse!

FIONA   Mum!

MOTHER   Well she won't stop, will she? She's enjoying herself too much.

FIONA   What's she doing now?

(MICHAEL *peeks.*)

MICHAEL   I can't really see, she might be crying.

MOTHER   Crocodile tears!

(MATILDA *begins packing some things into a bag.*)

MICHAEL   Mum, those things she said about me . . .

MOTHER   Lies son, all lies — Matilda is a LIAR Frank, it's all just LIES!

FIONA   It's true Dad, you know it is.

MICHAEL   Yes honest, Dad, you have to believe us!

FATHER   But why? Why? Why would she say these things?

MOTHER   Because she's not well, Frank.

FATHER   I want my little girl back.

MOTHER   Well let's try Frank, let's try and help her!

FATHER   It's too dangerous, it's too late.

MOTHER   Don't give up on her Frank, not yet. She's our
           daughter, we can help her!

FATHER   I'm frightened of her Mother!

MOTHER   We won't let her hurt you.

FIONA   No, we'll protect you Dad.

FATHER   Well we'll need some rope — we'll have to tie
           her up to restrain her — and something to cover
           her mouth.

MOTHER   Quick Michael, from out of the drawer. Hurry up!

FIONA   She's coming down.

           (MICHAEL *brings out a rope and gag as* MATILDA
           makes her way downstairs and out of the house.)

MOTHER   Quick Frank, hurry up!

FATHER   We'll all go together . . . stay close and act
           quickly . . . ready? After three . . . come on . . .
           One . . . two . . . three . . .

           (*They charge after her.* FATHER *jumps on her and
           then a noisy struggle as they drag her to a chair
           and bind and gag her against her will. They
           surround her menacingly.*)

MOTHER   Now then Matilda, just say you're sorry for all
           the lies and we'll say no more about it.

           (MOTHER *roughly pulls the gag away from*
           MATILDA'S *mouth.*)

MATILDA   (*trying*) I . . . can't!

MOTHER   We know it's hard to admit you're wrong but the
           things you've said — well they're awful and we
           think it's time you apologised — I mean it may
           not have been your fault, it may be that you're ill
           — don't you want to get better, is that it?

MATILDA   I want to, I want to, I just can't!

FIONA   For God's sake Matilda, say you're sorry, I've got things to do!

MATILDA   Well piss off and do them then!

MOTHER   Are you deliberately trying to upset your father?

FATHER   I thought she loved me.

MATILDA   I do love you but I have to tell the truth!

FIONA   I'll tell you the truth, you're an attention seeking little bitch, that's the truth!

MATILDA   What do you want me to do?

MICHAEL   Admit you lied.

MOTHER   And apologise.

MATILDA   I . . . eh . . . God save me!

FATHER   Maybe she's possessed.

MOTHER   My little girl possessed by the Devil!

FATHER   I think we ought to pray for her.

           (*They get on their knees and join hands.* MICHAEL *and* FIONA *look at each other,* FIONA *shrugs and they too join in the praying. They spit out their own vicious prayers into* MATILDA'S *ears while* FATHER *repeats* MOTHER'S.)

MOTHER   Forgive her Lord . . .

FATHER   Forgive her Lord . . .

MOTHER   Forgive her sins . . .

FATHER   Forgive her sins . . .

MOTHER   For she is the Devil's daughter . . .

ALL   For she is the Devil's daughter . . .

MATILDA   I'm not the Devil's daughter!

MOTHER   Out damned Satan! Out I say!

FIONA   Out damned Satan — out I say!

MOTHER   Dear Lord, save Matilda from the loathsome
               spirit that has entered her body — rid her of the
               demon that's bewitched her.

               (MICHAEL *moans.*)

MATILDA   FUCK OFF FIONA! Piss off Michael! It won't
               work! It won't work! MOTHER, IT WON'T
               WORK!!!!

               (*Suddenly they all stop praying.*)

FATHER   Why should we believe anything you say any
               more?

MATILDA   Because if you give me a proper chance I can
               prove to you that I don't tell lies.

FATHER   How will you prove it Matilda?

MATILDA   You'll have to untie my hands.

FATHER   I don't want you tricking me.

MATILDA   It's not a trick — I need free hands!

FATHER   Very well, but this had better be good.

               (MICHAEL *unties her hands but holds the noose of
               the rope towards her in case she tries to escape.
               She stands up and walks forward.*)

MATILDA   You wear a hair-piece, you are bald!

               (*She turns. The family look at each other in
               confusion.* MATILDA *walks towards* FATHER *and
               points. He looks bewildered. She rips off his wig
               and he stands there in genuine disbelief.*)

See? That's the truth!

FATHER That is not the truth! That is a lie! I'm not bald
. . . I'm not bald . . . *I'm not bald!*

MATILDA Of course you are — look!

(*She holds up the hair-piece.*)

FATHER I'm not bald . . . I'm not . . . Mother, am I bald?

MOTHER No Frank, you've got beautiful hair.

FATHER Fiona?

FIONA No Dad, you're not bald.

FATHER Michael?

MICHAEL (*shocked*) Eh . . . no, you're definitely not bald,
Dad.

FATHER You see? You have no proof!

MATILDA Get him a mirror — I've got your hair!

FATHER Can anybody see this hair she's raving on about?

ALL No.

MATILDA (*hysterical*) Look at the king! Look at the king!
Look at the king, the king, the king!

FATHER (*angry*) Get her! Get her!

(FIONA *chases* MATILDA *around the bottom of the
spiral staircase.* MOTHER *waits to catch her on the
way back.* FATHER *gets* MICHAEL *to help him drag
on a metal bath full of water as* MOTHER *and*
FIONA, *having caught her, hold her still as she
struggles to get free. It has become very vicious
and violent.*)

FATHER You see Matilda, you tell lies and you know what
happens to little girls who tell lies.

(They lift her up and duck her sharply under the water. They tug her head out dripping with water.)

Now, am I bald?

MATILDA   BALD AS A COOT!

(He forces her head under the water. They let her up spluttering.)

FATHER   NOW am I bald?

MATILDA   YES YOU'RE BALD AND STUPID AND FAT!

(They duck her under again furiously. MOTHER *begins counting, they join in turning it into a frantic chant.* MATILDA *is fighting to get out of the water but they hold her down. She hits the side of the bath, she feels for her* FATHER'S *body to grasp, she twitches and spasms and still they count as the life is nearly drained out of her body. They let her up and she collapses, spewing out water and fighting for air.)*

FATHER   *(pause)* Am I still bald?

(No answer.)

Have you stopped this nonsense?

(No answer.)

(inspecting her) Is he a fairy?

(No answer.)

Well I think she's stopped. Well done Princess. Quick Fiona get her a towel, she must be freezing. Mother, make her a hot cup of tea. Michael, help me move this back.

(FATHER and MICHAEL wheel the bath back to its position.)

FIONA   (*rubbing her down*) There you are Tillie, nearly dry.

MOTHER   I've made it nice and sweet, I know you like it sweet.

FATHER   What about our party tea? Shall we get the food back out?

(*They all cover their momentary shame by fussing over the party tea.* FIONA *gets out the wine and* MOTHER *the cake and all have one eye on* MATILDA *who sits dripping and pathetic on the floor.*)

MATILDA   I just want to say . . .

ALL   (*stopping dead*) Yes? Yes?

MATILDA   That I love you and I never meant to hurt you.

FIONA   Oh good . . .

MATILDA   BUT THE MAN'S A BALDY AND THE BOY'S A FAIRY, WHAT'S THE BIG . . . SHIT!

FATHER   GET HER! GET HER!

(*Everyone has screamed as* MATILDA *leaps up and makes a run for it around the spiral staircase. The family chase her in a frantic attempt to catch her as the lights change to silhouette. Amplified breathing, spotlight on* MATILDA *cowering in a corner with her eyes tightly shut.* FATHER'S *shadow moves across the stage. Others stampede rhythmically on the spot looking for her. Music fades in, "Adagio of Strings", and plays throughout the following scene.*)

FATHER   Hunted Matilda, hunted Matilda, who'll come a hunting Matilda with me? I can smell you, you've shit yourself. I can follow your stench, I can find you and when I do I'll rub your nose in it, dirty girl. I can hear your breathing, I can hear your heart beat. Shhhh, quietly now, you're leading me right to you. Boo!

MATILDA   AAAGGGGGHHHH!!!!!!!

(FIONA *and* MICHAEL *chase her behind the staircase, but they stay there out of sight. Only* MATILDA *appears again running around and around the space like a hunted animal, the pitter-patter of her feet sounds like her heart beating in panic. She looks fragile and haunted. She continues to run as* Mother *and* FATHER *watch and whisper each time she passes them.*)

FATHER   She looks pale.

MOTHER   She is pale.

(*They wait for her to come round again.*)

FATHER   She looks ill.

MOTHER   She is ill.

(*They wait again.*)

FATHER   She looks dead.

MOTHER   She is . . . dead.

FATHER   Burn her.

(FATHER *puts his arms around* MOTHER *and moves her out of* MATILDA'S *path.*)

Burn her!
Burn her!
Burn her!

(MOTHER *joins in, defeated.*)

Burn her!
Burn her!

(*Suddenly* FIONA *appears carrying a lighted torch.* MATILDA *recoils in horror. She turns and*

runs but MICHAEL *has entered from the other
direction also carrying a flame torch. She is
trapped from both exits as* FATHER *continues to
chant.*)

Burn her!
Go on, burn her!

(MATILDA *has nowhere to turn so she climbs the
tall ladder attached to the staircase. She reaches
the top and turns around but* MICHAEL *has
climbed the staircase and stands on the tower
behind the ladder waving the flame around her
dangerously.* FIONA *stands at the foot of the
ladder waving the flame at her feet.* MOTHER *and*
FATHER *stand huddled together watching,* FATHER
egging them on.)

FATHER   You see Matilda you tell lies and you know what
              happens to little girls who tell lies — BURN
              HER! BURN HER! BURN HER! BURN HER!
              And therefore when her Aunt returned Matilda
              and the house were burn her! Burn her! BURN
              HER!

              (MATILDA *is now panicking at the top of the
              ladder and suddenly starts shouting.*)

MATILDA   I was lying — I was lying — I was telling lies!

              (*As if to wake herself from this nightmare but too
              late.* MICHAEL *and* FIONA *have set her alight, the
              flames disappear as she is covered by a huge
              explosion of smoke rising from beneath her.*)

              NOOOOOOOOOOO!

              (*Her scream is animal. Through the smoke we see
              her face lit by a beam of light. Her eyes are
              looking to heaven and her lips mutter a prayer as
              the angelic music crescendos and the lights fade
              to black.*)

ACT THREE

The music begins to fade down as clock ticking takes over. A light fades up on MATILDA *who is standing in her room watching the scisors as she opens and closes them. Her hair is long again and the image repeats that at the end of Act One. Light cross fades out on* MATILDA *and up on the family sitting in their party hats at the table.* FIONA *enters as she did in the previous act, a mirror image of the beginning of Act Two.*

FATHER   SURPRISE!

FIONA   Hi Dad.

FATHER   Come in, come in. Mother, look who's here!

MOTHER   Fiona! What are you doing here? Frank, you haven't dragged her here for this?

FIONA   I wouldn't have missed it for the world. How are you Michael?

MICHAEL   Fine.

FIONA   Where's Matilda?

                (MOTHER *indicates* MATILDA'S *bedroom.*)

MOTHER   She spends all her time in there these days, reading children's books.

FATHER   Where are the children?

FIONA   At nursery school.

FATHER   Ah well, never mind — you'll see them soon Mother. We'll go up and visit one of these days.

FIONA   So! How's everything?

FATHER   Fine!

                (FIONA *can sense that it isn't.* MOTHER *and* MICHAEL *both look distracted.*)

FIONA   How is Matilda?

MOTHER ⎫   The same.
MICHAEL ⎬   A pain.
FATHER ⎭   Fine!

FIONA   I see. Is she not joining us then?

           (MICHAEL *and* MOTHER *shrug.*)

FATHER   MATILDA! Come on, we've a surprise for you
           out here!

FIONA   Don't get her excited Dad — she'll be
           disappointed it's only me.

FATHER   'Course she won't, she'll be thrilled to bits.

           (*There is an awkward pause as no one seems to
           know what to say to each other.*)

           Come on Tillie! We're waiting to get started!

           (FATHER *smiles at* FIONA *who politely smiles back.
           Another awkward pause. All at once they go to
           speak.*)

FATHER   I don't know if . . .

FIONA   So what's happening at . . .

MOTHER   Does anybody want . . .

ALL   Sorry . . .

FIONA   After you.

MOTHER   No, go on.

FIONA   I just wondered what's been happening lately.
           Any news?

           (*They all think about this but shake their heads.*)

MOTHER   Shall I get everyone a drink?

FATHER   No, I think we should wait for Matilda.

MOTHER   Well go and get her then Frank, this is ridiculous.

FATHER   She'll be out in a minute — don't push her all the time.

MOTHER   I'm not. Fiona hasn't come to sit and wait for Matilda.

FATHER   That's right — she's come to see her family, which is exactly what she is doing, I just don't want Matilda to miss out on the party.

MOTHER   I thought it was supposed to be Michael's party!

FATHER   It is for Michael, but we all should be together to celebrate . . . shouldn't we Michael?

MOTHER   MATILDA! Get out here now!

FATHER   Stop shouting.

MOTHER   She won't be able to hear if I don't shout.

MICHAEL   Can't we start without her — get it over with?

FATHER   What do you mean get it over with?

MOTHER   MATILDA!

MICHAEL   Here we go . . .

FATHER   No Michael, I want to know.

MOTHER   MATILDA!

MICHAEL   It doesn't matter Dad, honestly, we'll wait.

(FIONA *observes the family's tension.*)

MOTHER   She's doing it on purpose.

FATHER   Doing what?

MOTHER   Not coming out.

FIONA   (*pause*) What's been going on?

MOTHER   Matilda's still telling lies that's all, and your
            father thinks it's all great fun.

FIONA   What kind of lies?

MOTHER   The kind that embarrass us. She told a neighbour
            I was dead yesterday.

FIONA   Well why did she do that?

MOTHER   I don't know.

FATHER   She's just a bit rebellious.

FIONA   Well what is she rebelling against?

MOTHER   She's been the same ever since Michael's
            wedding. She hasn't stopped lying since then.

FIONA   Well, have you tried asking her why?

MOTHER   Oh she won't talk to me, and your father just
            encourages her.

FATHER   No I don't. You take everything too seriously.

FIONA   What about you Michael? Don't you talk to her?

MOTHER   He hasn't uttered a word to her since last year
            and I can't honestly say I blame him.

FIONA   Well it can't be very nice for Matilda.

MOTHER   Then she shouldn't have wrecked his marriage
            should she?

FIONA   I think Elaine wrecked his marriage Mum, she's
            the one who ran screaming down the aisle.

MICHAEL   Do we have to talk about this?

FATHER	I don't know why you're all so serious! Here she is, look! Hello, Princess — look who's here!

(MATILDA *has entered the sitting room. She looks very pale and unsteady on her feet.*)

FIONA	Are you alright Matilda?

FATHER	Of course she is. Come on then, sit down. Mother, you can go and fetch the drinks now.

(MATILDA *sits down, clutching the table.*)

FIONA	I think she's going to be sick.

FATHER	What's the matter Princess, don't you feel well?

(*Suddenly blood begins to pour from* MATILDA'S *mouth.*)

MATILDA! MATILDA!

(FATHER *is trying to bring her round. He opens her mouth and looks inside.*)

MOTHER	Frank . . . what is it . . . what?

FATHER	It's her tongue — she's lost her tongue!

MOTHER	What do you mean? FRANK! What's happened? MATILDA!

FATHER	Michael — get an ambulance — QUICKLY!

MOTHER	Ohhhh . . . Matilda, what have you done . . . no . . . no . . . no . . .

MICHAEL	Dad, don't let her bleed like that —

FATHER	GET TO THE PHONE!

MOTHER	No . . . no . . . no . . . no . . .

FATHER   Fiona — Go into her room — you've got to find it!

MOTHER   Oh no . . . no . . . no . . .

(MICHAEL *has rushed to make the phone call,* FATHER *is holding* MATILDA *trying to stop the blood,* FIONA *rushes to the bedroom to look for* MATILDA'S *tongue,* MOTHER *is trembling with shock. Music has faded in under the scene, "Adagio of Strings".*)

FATHER   Sssh, it's alright Matilda, you're going to be alright, sssh. Silly girl, eh? What have you done to yourself?

(*He looks up as* MICHAEL *enters.*)

FATHER   How long did they say?

MICHAEL   As soon as they can.

FATHER   Go and wait by the door — let me know as soon as it arrives.

(FIONA *comes in holding the scissors. They are bloodstained.*)

FIONA   She cut it off! Oh Dad . . .

FATHER   Did you find it?

FIONA   No . . . it's not there.

FATHER   You have to find it!

(FIONA *goes back into the bedroom, very distressed.*)

MOTHER   Let me hold her Frank, she's my daughter, let me hold her!

(FATHER *realises that* MATILDA *is dying.*)

FATHER   MICHAEL! Help me get her to the car.

MICHAEL   They'll be here soon, Dad.

FATHER   Help me get her to the car! We can't waste any
               more time.

               (MICHAEL *and* FATHER *carry her now unconscious*
               body outside with MOTHER *sobbing after them.*
               FIONA *runs out of* MATILDA'S *room and round and*
               round the space, eyes darting frantically for the
               tongue. As she runs her hands shake violently in
               front of her, the pitter-patter of her feet is a
               horrible mirror of the sound of panic. She keeps
               running until there is nowhere else to look and
               collapses in a chair. Lights fade to blackout.
               Music continues in the dark. When the lights rise,
               MOTHER, FATHER *and* MICHAEL *are entering the*
               house from the hospital. FIONA *looks at* MOTHER
               but MOTHER *just shakes her head.* MOTHER *is very*
               pale and drawn, they all take up various
               positions of defeat and fatigue. they still wear the
               party hats, although a couple of them have now
               dropped off or become wonky. They all look
               shattered. The pain that all of them are feeling is
               tangible.)

FIONA   I don't understand it . . .

MICHAEL   What time have we got to ring up?

FATHER   They said give it a couple of hours.

MICHAEL   I can't stand the waiting.

FIONA   I just don't understand. Why did she do it?

               (*There is a pause, the question hanging in the*
               air.)

MOTHER   I burned her books.

FIONA   What books?

MOTHER   Her favourite books. I burned them.

FIONA   Why?

MOTHER   I wish I hadn't . . .

FIONA   She wouldn't have done it because of that — she
               didn't even know you'd burned them, did she?

MOTHER   (*inaudibly*) I don't know.

FATHER   Oh Matilda . . . Matilda . . . I need a whisky —
               anyone?

               (*They shake their heads. He doesn't move.*)

MOTHER   What time is it?

FATHER   Not time yet.

MOTHER   I should be there.

FATHER   There's no point . . . they asked us to leave, it
               wasn't my idea.

MOTHER   I should have stayed.

FATHER   We can go later.

FIONA   I feel really sick.

FATHER   Shall I get you some water?

FIONA   No.

               (*Slight pause.*)

MICHAEL   I love Matilda.

FATHER   We . . . we all do son.

MICHAEL   It's your fault.

FATHER   Don't be silly.

MICHAEL   It's your fault.

FATHER   Son, it's nobody's fault.

MICHAEL   It's YOUR fault!

FATHER   Michael . . .

MICHAEL   She was right and we denied it.

MOTHER   Shut up, Michael.

MICHAEL   (*to* MOTHER) You thought you could put me right,
              you thought Elaine would put me right.

MOTHER   (*through tears*) Don't you think we've had
              enough for one day without you being stupid?

MICHAEL   It doesn't matter any more, it really doesn't. I
              don't care any more!

FATHER   You're not making sense son — you're confused.

MICHAEL   I'm not confused — I'm gay!

FIONA   Jesus Christ!

MICHAEL   Shut up.

FIONA   Well, Michael — how do you know?

MICHAEL   What do you mean how do I know? Elaine knew
              too — as soon as Matilda said it — Elaine knew.

MOTHER   I don't have to listen to this (*She goes to move.*)

MICHAEL   Yes you do! You've never cared about us, you've
              only cared about yourself.

FATHER   Don't speak to your mother like that!

MICHAEL   DON'T speak to your mother like that, DO speak
              to your father like this — just be what they want
              — do as you're told and pretend, lie, deny,
              because if you don't they won't love you any
              more!

FATHER   Is that what you think? Is that what you think?
            Michael!

MICHAEL   Yes!

MOTHER   But you're not.

MICHAEL   But I am!

FIONA   You coward.

MICHAEL   You bitch!

FATHER   Eh! That's enough! Matilda is who we should be
            thinking about —

MICHAEL   Matilda is who I am thinking about! I thought
            she'd wrecked my life. I hated her for it.

MOTHER   We all hated her for it.

FATHER   I didn't. I love Matilda, I love you all, whatever
            you do.

MOTHER   Because you don't understand Frank. You don't
            understand about caring for your children, being
            responsible for their welfare. Left to you they'd
            all end up in cuckoo land. People don't take
            kindly to what Michael says he is, you don't
            know what people will do to him.

MICHAEL   And neither do you! You both want to control us
            all the time.

FIONA   Well you should have got on with your life
            Michael, nobody forced you to get married.

MICHAEL   Didn't they? Just because it happened to be what
            you wanted didn't mean you had a choice.

FIONA   Well I think you've got a lot to answer for.
            Matilda did it because of you and I'll tell you
            what Michael, I wouldn't like to be in your shoes.

MICHAEL   You've hardly been around, you don't know what
           it's like here. You ran away from this family
           Fiona, so don't start preaching to me!!

FIONA   Is it any wonder I ran away from people who
           won't confront anything? Look at you all —
           you've let this happen — you've let Matilda
           mutilate herself!

FATHER   I don't know what you're trying to say —
           Matilda's always been happy here.

FIONA   Oh, grow up Dad!

FATHER   Mother — can you understand this?

MOTHER   My name's not Mother, Frank — it's Lilian! It's
           always been Lilian!

FATHER   Look you're upsetting your mother now . . .

MOTHER   Oh that's it — blame the kids — it's you who
           upsets me Frank, you're the one who's turned
           Michael out like this — what weird stories have
           you been putting into their heads all these years?

MICHAEL   Nobody turned me out like "this"!

MOTHER   How do you know Michael? How do I know?

FIONA   There's nothing wrong with being gay these days
           anyway, Mother — everybody is.

MOTHER   Are you?

FIONA   No, I'm not.

MOTHER   Well shut up then!

MICHAEL   Oh what's the point. My sister might be dying
           and all you care about is what the neighbours
           might say.

MOTHER   Fuck the neighbours! Fuck the neighbours! I've
           never had a whole day to myself, do you know

that? I've had to worry about you from day one. When he tells you his stories about princes and princesses — he doesn't tell you that they shag you, impregnate you, lock you in the castle and throw away the key! My life has been one big shock to me — I expected to enjoy it!! The least you could have done was turned out well for my efforts and you! You could have taken a bit more responsibility so the whole thing didn't always end up on my shoulders!

FATHER   I've done my best. My very very best.

MOTHER   Well I don't think either of us have done a good enough job Frank.

FATHER   Oh don't say that . . . please don't say that.

FIONA   Mother — please! You've been everything to us, you've been here day in and day out — you've never given up on us — never stopped fighting for us and we think you're FUCKING BRILLIANT! We think you're a BRILLIANT mother and a BRILLIANT person — I couldn't do what you've done, I haven't got the guts and strength, but you can't sit back and suffer and sacrifice because all that does is spread misery — you've got to get up off your backside and KNOW that you're FUCKING BRILLIANT so we can all stop feeling so fucking guilty for making you unhappy — YOU make you unhappy — and you don't deserve it, alright? So please, can we ring the hospital!

FATHER   No, let's go down there — we've a right to know what's happening.

(FATHER *nervously approaches* MOTHER *and* MICHAEL.)

It's alright son . . . we love you, don't we . . . Lilian . . . yeah . . . 'course we do.

(FATHER *and* FIONA *exit quickly leaving* MICHAEL *and* MOTHER *alone.*)

MICHAEL   Mum, just because we've been fooling ourselves doesn't mean you haven't done a good job — I know it's not what you wanted for me — it's not what I had in mind for myself. But if you let me I can still be a son to you.

MOTHER   I want to see Matilda — I'm going to see MATILDA!

(*She leaves.* MICHAEL *looks rejected and shocked. He puts on his jacket as he reflects on the situation. He makes his way up to* MATILDA'S *room and picks up her book. He turns and looks into her imaginary mirror.*)

MICHAEL   When I was a boy, what did they teach me? The difference between right and wrong, not to lie, the other nine commandments. They taught me 'cause I was lucky, how to spell, add up, algebra, Pythagoras's theorem, they told me how to write a letter, read a book, decipher a poem, they told me that William the Conqueror invaded us in 1066, they told me they grow tea in India and cocoa beans in Jamaica, and they told me to run round the school in my knickers and vest. They didn't tell me how to deal with hate, they didn't even tell me that I was likely to experience it often in life, that when I felt frustrated or depressed or like bottling someone's face in, how to handle my emotions. They didn't teach me how not to explode, they didn't teach me the power of positive thinking, they didn't teach me to tolerate, fight, survive! They didn't teach me how to negotiate danger, or that it's ok to feel like shit, to be confused. They didn't tell me how not to go crazy, cope with cancer, cure the blues! They just taught me the important things in life, those things I draw on again and again when the going gets tough! Thou shalt not sin and thou shalt learn thy twelve times table by heart by Monday or else! Other lessons in life should be

learned when it's too late, through experience
when you're in prison 'cause you've snapped and
stabbed if you're lazy enough to get depressed,
bad enough to get angry, weird enough to feel
different, those lessons are not for us, not for us!

(MICHAEL *has finished with his arms raised above
his head. He catches his own reflection and
smiles, dropping his arms to his side. He is still
holding* MATILDA'S *book which he opens. As he
does the light bulb shines on his face from its
pages and her voice fills the space as lights fade
down on* MICHAEL.)

MATILDA'S   Meanwhile in the forest Matilda was on
VOICE   horseback, she was galloping across the wooded
world where her lover was skinny dipping, she
spied him in the far-off lake and kicked the horse
on faster. His naked body was glistening as he
heard the rumble of hooves and the sunlight lit
his lashes as he blinked in wonder at the
approaching vision. She rode with all her might
as the wind blew through her hair and she
scooped him up on route and he wrapped his legs
around her. The two went galloping on until they
reached their destination, a world with women
writing stories and children asking questions and
men crying out in joy and pain. As she looked
across the wood to the world from which she'd
galloped, she tilted her head skywards and
thanked the stars above, that she was free at last.

The End.